ONE IN A BILLION

Dear Sarah Jane,

my Journey is one in a billion because you've been a part of it Thank you for always believing in me.

Much love,
Sonal — ♡

SONAL C HOLLAND

ONE IN A BILLION

BECOMING INDIA'S FIRST MASTER OF WINE

WESTLAND
BUSINESS

WESTLAND
BUSINESS

Published by Westland Business, an imprint of Westland Books, a division of Nasadiya Technologies Private Limited, in 2025

No. 269/2B, First Floor, 'Irai Arul', Vimalraj Street, Nethaji Nagar, Alapakkam Main Road, Maduravoyal, Chennai 600095

Westland, the Westland logo, Westland Business and the Westland Business logo are the trademarks of Nasadiya Technologies Private Limited, or its affiliates.

ISBN: 9789360456467

10 9 8 7 6 5 4 3 2 1

The views and opinions expressed in this work are the author's own and the facts are as reported by her, and the publisher is in no way liable for the same.

Typeset by Jojy Philip

Printed at Thomson Press (India) Ltd

To Papa,
my first champion, whose quiet strength and unwavering belief
in me lit the path to the stars, forever inspiring me to reach
beyond what I ever imagined possible.

Contents

Prologue: The Third Best Day of My Life   1

The Call that Changed Everything
Penny Richards, Former Executive Director,
The Institute of Masters of Wine   6

1.   Ordinary Circumstances, Extraordinary Parents   7

2.   Ticket to the Rollercoaster   19

'I couldn't have asked for more ...'
Speech by Sonal's father at her wedding   25

3.   'You Should Be Like Her'   27

4.   New Kid on the Block   38

Early Years, and Sonal Dives into Wine
Rekha Chandole, Sonal's mother   54

5.   London Calling   57

Sonal Endears Herself to Everyone She Meets
Chris Holland, Sonal's stepson   67

Sonal's Reinvention of Herself
Charlotte Holland, Sonal's stepdaughter   68

6. She's Definitely Mine   69

    A Daughter's Opinion
    Rianna, Sonal and Andrew's daughter   80

7. If Not Me, Then Who?   81

8. Two Hundred Wines and a Wedding   92

    'And then there's Sonal ...'
    Richard Hemming MW, a friend of Sonal's   102

9. When the Going Gets Tough   104

10. Tastebuds on Fire   116

11. Winner's Mindset   132

    The Face of Indian Wine
    Andrew Holland, Sonal's husband   143

12. Tasting Success One Sip at a Time   147

13. Building a Personal Brand   156

    A Sister's View
    Rimal D'Silva, Sonal's sister   169

14. Riding the India Growth Wave   172

15. Woman in a Man's World   181

    'The galaxy is the limit ...'
    Sharmin Photographer, Sonal's childhood friend   187

Epilogue: Life Comes Full Circle   189

Acknowledgements   194

PROLOGUE

The Third Best Day of My Life

It's 6 September 2016, my Mumbai home is bustling with joy and energy—it is Ganesh Chaturthi. Preparations are in full swing to celebrate the arrival of Lord Ganesha. We have duly adorned the main door with a toran—auspicious mango leaves strung together—and drawn a pretty rangoli under it to welcome the Lord. My parents, sister, brother-in-law and niece too are visiting to celebrate the festival with us.

This festival is a yearly ritual for us, a tradition I have inherited from my parents and continue to celebrate with a lot of enthusiasm. While we were growing up, we would decorate our home on this auspicious day, dress up in finery, perform puja, distribute prasad, and then, after a heady three days, send off Ganapati with tears in our eyes.

There's something about Ganesh Chaturthi that fills you with joy and excitement, and it's impossible to stay immune to the festive spirit in Mumbai. I, however, am a nervous wreck today— my results from the Master of Wine exam are due to arrive. I have spent a decade building credentials that will shape my career in the world of wine, the last six of which have gone into chasing the wine world's most coveted title: Master of Wine (MW). This chase has pushed me to my breaking point, kept me away from my daughter and husband for months on end, not to mention, cost a fortune and made me question every single life decision. And today I will get to know the outcome of it all.

I have good reason to be at my wit's end; passing the exam is nearly next to impossible. The Institute of Masters of Wine (IMW) in the UK doesn't reveal the exact pass rate for each batch of students, but it is almost as low as that for the Indian Civil Services Examination, which is usually a single-digit number. The MW is the highest qualification in the world of wine. Consider this: way more people have scaled Mount Everest or travelled to space than have become Master of Wine (only about 512 since 1953).[1]

No one from India has yet achieved this distinction. Most MWs come from prominent wine-producing regions and markets like the UK, the US, Australia, New Zealand, Spain, France, etc. Even Italy, one of the most prominent winemaking regions in the world, didn't have an MW in 2016. Asian countries like China and Singapore, both bustling wine markets, have just a couple of MWs. So how could a woman from India dare to even dream about it, coming from a country where the per capita consumption of wine is less than a teaspoon?

The Institute of Masters of Wine has a three-stage programme—the first round is a preliminary exam, the second is the main exam consisting of theory and blind-tasting papers and the third is a 10,000-word research paper. Only after clearing all three stages does one receive the coveted certification. I have already cleared the first two stages and am on the last leg of the qualification. While I can see the finish line, you never know when you slip on your way to the title.

---

[1] 'About Us', *The Institute of Masters of Wine*, https://www.mastersofwine.org/about-us/faqs.

If I pass, I will become the first Indian MW. This will not only make me the ultimate authority on the subject of wine in the country, but also give me unparalleled access to some of the best wine-related events, networks and communities in the world. It will also validate all the sacrifices that I have made in the last decade. It is easy to weave a narrative around a victory, but how do you find meaning in failure? If I fail, do the last six years of my life get reduced to nothing? How do I justify all that expense and effort? This is going to be the first day of the rest of my life, either as a failed MW student or as India's first MW. The wait is making me dizzy.

I keep checking my watch as we prepare for the Ganapati puja. Every time a phone rings in the house, my heart skips a beat. The panditji signals to me that it is time to start the ceremony, but before I can proceed, my mother puts her hand gently on my shoulder and says, 'Sonal, forget about everything else for the next hour and devote yourself to Ganesha. He comes just once a year and he should have your undivided attention.'

I nod in agreement and say, 'Yes Mummy. But if I get a call in the middle of the puja, we will have to stop the proceedings because I can't miss it. In fact, I think the Lord would want me to take that call.'

My mother raises her hands in submission and tells the priest to proceed. I try to focus on the puja with all my heart, but the fear rumbling in my stomach is too distracting. Then, at 10.30 a.m., my phone rings. I go numb. My hands work from muscle memory to take the call, as my legs carry me to a nearby window for better reception. With my back to my family and my heart in my mouth, I put the phone to my ear.

On the other end is Penny Richards, the then Executive Director of IMW. Penny, usually very friendly, sounds formal and distant: 'Hi, this is Penny Richards calling from the Institute of

Masters of Wine. Is this Sonal Holland?' For seven decades, this institute has been recognised globally for its rigour and exacting standards. Anyone representing the institute is sure to feel the weight of its legacy on their shoulders, and her tone reflects this.

It is as if someone has stolen my voice—I can barely speak. Finally, I manage a hoarse 'Hi.' I want Penny to skip the pleasantries and just put me out of my misery. Luckily, she does just that.

'Hi Sonal, I am calling to let you know that your research paper has been accepted and you are now officially a Master of Wine.'

The first words out of my mouth are, 'Are you serious?'

Penny's tone immediately changes, and she goes back to being her friendly self: 'Of course I am serious, Sonal! Why else do you think I am calling you at 6 a.m. from the UK? I am so happy to be waking up to this news, and you know what? You are the first one I've called. I'll be calling up the rest of the world soon.'

Joy, relief, excitement and gratitude—all these emotions leave me speechless. It is over, finally. I have done it!

As I turn around with tears in my eyes, I see my family waiting for me to break the news. Achieving this distinction wouldn't have been possible without their support, and they are as invested in this journey as I am.

'So are you going to tell us or what?' Andrew asks.

'It has happened, guys. I am now a Master of Wine!'

The house erupts with joy as I touch my parents' feet, hug my sister and kiss my husband. Meanwhile, the panditji looks befuddled by the commotion. Although he is sure that it won't be over soon, he still graciously gives us a few more minutes to celebrate before requesting us to finish the puja. He is a busy man after all, especially today, and Bappa is waiting for him at other homes too.

Another person in the room is puzzled by this sudden interruption in the rituals and the loud commotion that has followed. My seven-year-old daughter Rianna looks confused as to why I am crying and laughing at once. To see me cry with such abandon is new to her.

'What's going on, Daddy? What happened to Mumma?' she asks.

I started my MW journey when my daughter was just a year old and so far, she has only seen her mother studying or absconding for weeks at a time. She knew that I was working hard, but was too young to understand what was at stake for me.

'Rianna, you remember how Mummy has been constantly travelling and studying all this time? She had to stay away from you because she was taking this really difficult exam. She just got to know that she passed it. She is the only one in India to become a Master of Wine. You must give Mummy a big hug and congratulate her,' Andrew tells her.

My daughter walks up to me, wraps her arms around my neck and asks, 'Mummy, is it true? Are you the only Master of Wine in all of India?'

'Yes beta, that is true,' I say.

Rianna, who is in grade two and is learning numbers in school, quickly does the math and exclaims, 'Oh wow, Mummy! That makes you one in a billion.'

The enormity of my achievement suddenly sinks in. In all these years that I aimed to become India's first Master of Wine, never once did I stop to think that it will make me unique among a billion people.

I hug my daughter tightly and say, 'Thank you, Riu! You've just given Mummy the best compliment and greatest tagline, ever.'

The Call that Changed Everything
Penny Richards, Former Executive Director,
The Institute of Masters of Wine

I still remember calling Sonal to let her know she had become a Master of Wine. She was always such an inspiring candidate at the Institute of Masters of Wine, and quickly became a dedicated and generous Member of the magnificent organisation. And it's now a complete delight to watch her inspiring a whole new community of wine lovers in India and beyond. I couldn't be more proud to know her, and enjoy a glass with her whenever possible.

1

Ordinary Circumstances, Extraordinary Parents

Since I became a Master of Wine, I have been given credit for successfully reinventing my career and pivoting from my cushy corporate job with a seven-figure salary to a career in wine, which was yet to grow and enjoy the popularity that it does today. While people admire this move, many assume I was primed for success from an early age. They look at the superficial trappings of my current life and assume that I was born to rich parents and have always lived a fancy life, studying at the best schools and Ivy League colleges that have given me a head-start in my career. From their perspective, the Master of Wine title is a result of my prosperous upbringing. However, I didn't achieve this level of success in my career because I came from an influential family or had a vast inheritance at my disposal to give me a jumpstart.

I grew up in a lower-middle-class family. Up to the age of thirty-one, I lived in the Reserve Bank Colony near Maratha Mandir at Mumbai Central. My father worked for the Reserve Bank of India while my mother was employed with the Brihanmumbai Municipal Corporation. My sister and I were raised in a one-bedroom-hall-kitchen (1 BHK) house, which was eventually replaced by a 2 BHK quarter as my father rose through the ranks.

We never had the disposable income for fine dining or luxury holidays. I had never stepped into a five-star restaurant until I began a career in hospitality, and our idea of entertainment over the weekends was to catch a movie at the Ganga or Jamuna Cinema in Tardeo, followed by a meal at restaurants like Sardar Pav Bhaji or the local Udupi.

Despite our limited means, our family found many ways to fill our lives with joy. For instance, my parents made a huge deal about the festive season—my sister Rimal and I would get new clothes every Diwali, and we would decorate our house with marigold flowers and diyas. My mother would cook delicious faral delicacies that were duly exchanged with relatives and neighbours.

We would celebrate Ganesh Chaturthi at my eldest uncle's home, where all the seven brothers, including my father, their wives and as many as twenty of my cousins would gather for the festival. The entire family would live under one roof for a week-long celebration. While my uncle's apartment was not big enough to house so many, he would host us with a lot of love and enthusiasm. The twenty of us would raise a riot, feasting on festive delicacies, playing through the day and chatting late into the night. Because of these wonderful memories, Ganesh Chaturthi remains a special festival to me even today, and I make sure my daughter and husband experience it the same way I used to as a child.

Being an only child for a long time, I was the centre of my parents' universe. They showered me with immense love and care, and instilled great confidence in me. However, behind the enthusiasm they showed in celebrating my every little milestone was unbearable pain.

When I was four years old, my mother gave birth to my sister Monal. Before she even turned one, Monal fell very sick. My parents later suspected that she suffered from a devastating combination of Type 1 diabetes and lactose intolerance, which went undetected. They tried their best to save Monal and, in the process, they didn't have a lot of time for me. There were days when my parents would drop me at my grandparents' house in the middle of the night before taking my sister to the hospital. I often slept in class and lost a lot of weight as I wasn't eating well; I only learnt about all this later from them. My parents ran from pillar to post to get Monal adequate medical care, but, despite their best efforts, she passed away before she turned one.

One evening after her passing is still etched in my memory— the three of us were sitting in the bedroom of our matchbox-sized flat. I don't know what they were talking about but suddenly, Mummy and Daddy began to cry inconsolably, mourning my sister's death. I was too small to understand the depth of their grief; parents crying their hearts out is something that no child wants to see. Soon, I felt tears rolling down my cheeks as my parents held me tight like I was the most treasured thing in their lives. It was as if they could afford to lose anything at that point in life except me.

I remember my father saying, 'Now we must take good care of her.'

At that moment, the only thought that came to my mind was that I wanted to make them happy, no matter what.

After this incident, I received undivided attention from my parents till my younger sister Rimal came along. They took utmost care of me, making sure I ate well, taking me for regular check-ups so that I remained in the pink of health. It became their life's mission to give me the best possible upbringing. I could always see unconditional pride and love for me in their eyes. They always encouraged me to do well and gave me immense confidence in my capabilities.

My father's progressive thinking set our household apart from those around us. He aspired for us to have a promising future despite our ordinary circumstances. He laid great emphasis on good education, as he firmly believed that as long as you keep learning, you keep rising. To this day, I am a strong advocate of upskilling for better career opportunities, thanks to the conditioning he provided me in my formative years.

This was a time when girls' education in Bombay was free, and my father utilised this opportunity to enrol his daughters at the Convent of Jesus & Mary St Agnes' High School. So while many of my friends went to a Marathi-medium school within the colony premises because it was convenient for their parents, my sister and I went to a convent school some distance away. In the 1970s, sending your children to a convent school was a huge deal for middle-class parents as they believed it would help their children gain additional skills as well as aid their personality development, apart from giving them a good education in English. That's what my parents wanted for their daughters.

I was good at studies, although I was quite a mischief-maker in school. I never had any sense of worry or responsibility while growing up, but which child does? Since I was good at academics, I often got away with pranks that would have otherwise landed me in the principal's office.

For instance, in the tenth standard, I pranked my maths teacher by covering every inch of the blackboard with a fine layer of candle wax. The teacher was flabbergasted as the chalk kept slipping off the board when she tried to write on it, and the students couldn't stop chuckling. While no one ratted me out at that moment, she eventually found out and complained to the principal. I could have been suspended for my actions, but it was the last year of school and we were just a few months away from our board exams, so the principal let it slide and simply asked me to apologise to my teacher, which I did.

However, the teacher was in no mood to forgive me. She looked into my eyes and said, 'I'd like to see your face when the results come out.' She expected me to either fail or perform badly in the exams. But when the results came, I passed with flying colours, even securing a place among the top ten ranking students from our school. I was the one having the last laugh!

Despite having the intellect to do well academically, I neither had the discipline nor the commitment to excel at anything and was rather committed to being a rogue. This trait led to a graceless fall in college.

I secured admission to the Science stream at St Xavier's College with my SSC exam result. My parents were overjoyed as they wanted me to become a doctor. But their joy didn't last long. Within two years, I had slipped in studies and attendance, to the extent that the college asked me to take admission elsewhere for my bachelor's degree. While my parents were not pleased about this, they secured a spot for me at Kishinchand Chellaram College. Just six months later, however, I marched back home and announced that I had switched from Science to Arts. Without consulting my parents, I had gone to the administration office to get my name moved to another stream in their records. The reason? I had made some friends in the Arts stream and wanted to hang out with them. My parents were extremely disappointed—I could never be a doctor now.

The friends in question were a bad influence on me. I bunked college to watch movies with them and would spend hours talking to them on the phone. My spending had also gone out of control and my daily allowance of ₹20 a day was simply not enough. Not one to settle for less, I started demanding more money from my mother to buy clothes and to spend on outings with my friends.

My mother worked at the Brihanmumbai Municipal Corporation headquarters in Victoria Terminus (now Chhatrapati Shivaji Terminal). My college was just down the road. Whenever I needed extra pocket money, I barged into her office, much to her embarrassment. She felt other women around her had demure daughters who helped with household chores, spoke softly and dressed 'appropriately'. I, on the other hand, was never prim and proper, and my dressing style irked my mom. With limited pocket money, my only shopping avenue was Fashion Street as the clothes there were cheap and it was close to my college. I often chose clothes without understanding how they looked on me. The combinations I came up with made my mother dread crossing paths with me in public. Amongst other things I owned, I was really fond of a black polo neck top and a mini skirt. I often repeated this outfit, thinking they were the best pair of clothes I had. However, my mom detested the outfit. The minute she saw me approach her desk dressed like that, she would quickly take out her purse and hand me the money just to get me out of her colleagues' sight. However, she would reprimand me later and ask me to never come to her office again.

My mother's friends had many reasons apart from my clothes to despise me. I was a tomboy with a lot of male friends. In a conservative setup like ours, always hanging out with boys was seen as problematic, even if I wasn't romantically involved with any of them. My behaviour scandalised the gossip-mongering aunties in our colony, who used all their imagination to paint me as a wayward teen—*ladki haath se nikal gai*, the girl has got out of hand.

This behaviour earned me a certain reputation in the RBI colony. I only found out about this later, when a couple of my childhood friends told me that their parents had forbidden them from hanging out with me as they feared their children too would become rebellious. As hilarious as it sounds now, I cannot imagine what my poor mother endured because of my bindaas personality.

Then there was the non-stop partying, which gave my mother sleepless nights. Every night at eight, she would sit in the living room, her eyes shifting between the door to my bedroom and the main door, as she wondered where I was headed that night and with whom.

She would stand on the balcony every night, refusing to sleep, eagerly watching every cab that passed down the road outside our society, hoping that I would emerge. She could see her talented child throwing away her life and was worried about me. I must applaud my parents for their endless patience during this phase of my life. Any other parents would have dealt sternly with their child in such a situation. But my mother and father never raised their voice, or hit me, or grounded me or cut off my pocket money. They didn't threaten to halt my education or to marry me off to the first guy to come their way. Despite all the trouble I caused, Mummy and Daddy never forced their decisions on me.

The first year of college was when my life unravelled. My carefree attitude transitioned from being cute to cool and then, concerning. I paid no attention to my studies and barely attended college; my attendance was around five per cent. However, my absence from classes and the college campus caused much bigger damage than merely falling behind in academics, as I would soon find out.

I showed up to write my exams and couldn't find my roll number on the roster. I went to the admin office to enquire about this, thinking it was an error at their end. 'Excuse me, I am supposed to write my first-year exam today. But my roll number isn't on the list. Can you please check?' I said to the office personnel. He asked for my name and then flipped through one of the many thick folders lying in front of him.

'Your name isn't on the college roster anymore.'

'What? Why? Please check again.'

'You haven't paid your tuition fee. You are no longer a student of this college.'

It felt like a lightning bolt had hit me. I couldn't believe that I could have made such a gross error—I had missed out on the date to pay the next instalment of the fees. The college administration had put up multiple reminders about this on the notice board, but since I never attended classes, I hadn't come across them.

So, I lied. 'That's not possible. I paid my fee on time.'

'Okay, show me the receipt then,' he demanded.

I called my mother and asked her to find the receipt for the payment. Naturally, she couldn't. Since the exam was happening as we were speaking, my parents immediately came to the college and requested to meet the principal.

'There seems to be some confusion. Looks like Sonal forgot to tell us about the due date,' my father reasoned with him. 'We are willing to pay the penalty for the late fee, but please allow our daughter to write her exams. She is a very intelligent student; this would ruin her year.'

But the principal wasn't in the mood to overlook my error. 'Mr Chandole,' he said sternly. 'This isn't just about a missed payment. Are you aware that your daughter has less than five per cent attendance? Ask her how many lectures she attended last year, or how many assignments she completed. Why would I want to have a student like her in my college? Please take her and go somewhere else.'

My parents were stunned. While they knew I had been neglecting my studies, they had no idea things had got so bad. Nonetheless, they pleaded with the principal to change his decision, but to no avail. In the end, they could do nothing but bring me home.

From being an SSC topper to scoring 63.5 per cent in my class twelfth board exams to being thrown out of college in my first year because of poor attendance, it felt like my life had flipped on its head in the blink of an eye.

Watching my parents plead with the college administration was the wake-up call I needed. My humiliation didn't bother me, but to see my parents, my anchors, in such a helpless state deeply angered me. I was furious, but what could I do? It wasn't possible to go back to college, as that ship had sailed. Till that point in my life, I had been a happy-go-lucky girl who thought her actions would never have consequences. But I knew things had to change now.

My father didn't talk to me after the incident. I had hit rock bottom, and there was really nothing left to say. It pained me to see him go quiet and I felt terrible for disappointing him. But here's the thing about loving parents—they never give up on their children.

Despite feeling let down, Daddy found a way out for me and filled out a form in my name to sit for the National Council for Hotel Management and Catering Technology Joint Entrance Exam (NCHMCT-JEE). At that time, the hospitality industry was considered almost at par with the airline industry. It attracted good talent because it provided a sophisticated work environment. My father thought that if I managed to get into hotel management, I would get to work in an environment that would change my life for the better.

When he told me about the test, my mother sat me down and patiently told me, 'Sonal, you are in a terrible situation. Right now, you have two options—if you want the world to see you in such a miserable state, don't do anything about it. But if you want to turn your life around, then you need to study hard for these exams. Passing this test is your chance to cover up for your failure and start afresh.'

For once, I took her advice and immersed myself in my studies. I had to hit the reset button if I wanted to change the course of my future. I had five weeks to prepare for the test and I gave it my all. My sincerity also helped break the ice between me and my father. He saw that I was working hard to overcome the setback that I had received and that I had finally learnt from my past mistakes—I had realised that I needed to take my studies seriously if I wanted to succeed in life.

Five weeks of intense hard work bore fruit. I was selected in 1992 for the Institute of Hotel Management, Catering Technology and Applied Nutrition in Dadar, Mumbai—one of India's most prestigious hotel management institutes. I felt like life had given me a second chance. I was not going to throw away this lifeboat.

Once I got into IHM Mumbai, I was more careful. I was done with bunking classes. In all honesty, IHM runs a tight ship, and if you want to ace the course, you cannot afford to miss any classes. However, I didn't have much free time for another reason—I had decided to pursue my BA degree online. The hotel management course was enough to move my career forward, but sometimes, you do things purely for vindication. My parents' humiliation when I was thrown out of college had hurt me deeply and I wanted to get a BA degree to close a painful chapter of my life. Doing that would be my way of telling the world, and myself, that a 'lost cause' like me could turn her life around. So, I would spend my day running from one lecture to another at IHM Mumbai and then come home and study for both courses.

While I was good at studies, I was certainly not the most popular student at the institute. I don't think the professors were looking at me and thinking, 'This girl will achieve remarkable success one day.' However, I was hungry to learn and imbibe everything in the excellent environment that the institute created around me, and it inspired me to excel.

I emerged as the topper in the F&B course and received a lot of appreciation for my oral communication skills. I completed the three-year hotel management course and graduated with a BA degree in the same year. In 1995, I landed a job as a management trainee in the Taj Group of Hotels and was posted at the President Hotel in Cuffe Parade. My first salary was ₹3,000. While it wasn't much, it offered me a fresh start.

However, I quickly realised that the F&B sector required a lot of hard work and the financial rewards weren't proportional to the amount of work expected. After eight months of service, I considered quitting. But having learnt from my past mistakes, I decided to run my decision by my father first, who knew I wasn't happy with my work.

'Papa, I'm not happy with this job. It's too much work for too little money. But I'm not sure where to go from here.'

He heard me out patiently and said, 'Why don't you do an MBA?'

'Oh God! Two more years of studying! When will I make money?'

'Sonal, what do I always tell you? There is no better way to boost your career than through education. Don't worry about the money or how old you'll be when you get a job. Just think of how a post-graduate degree will increase your employability. You will earn more money than whatever you can get now as a graduate. Think of this as an investment that would become a great career advantage in the future.'

Management courses were becoming popular at the time in India. But the only reason I agreed to pursue a Master of Management Studies (MMS) course was that my best friend signed up for it too. Even if the reason was somewhat frivolous, this was definitely the right decision for me at that stage.

2

Ticket to the Rollercoaster

Finally, at the age of twenty-five, after completing the management course, I secured my first proper job at the Oberoi Towers in 1998 as a sales executive. My salary went from ₹3,000 to ₹8,000. While it wasn't significant financial growth, this was the point at which the trajectory of my career and personal life completely changed.

My father was elated with this appointment, as he had always wanted me to work in a space where I would be surrounded by people who would inspire me to become a more refined version of myself. If I worked in an environment which was better than my current reality, he believed, it would condition me to aim higher in life.

The Oberoi Towers introduced me to a sophisticated work culture that opened a whole new world for me. I used to wear my mom's silk sarees along with faux pearl necklaces so that I looked the part of a sales and marketing professional working on the carpeted executive floor. The unique combination of hotel management and MMS degrees gave me an understanding of consumer service and corporate culture. This, along with my communication skills, helped me settle down in my new job quickly.

Back in the day, the Oberoi Towers' lobby was dominated by a large staircase that gave it an air of grandeur. Every time I walked down it, I felt as if the world was my oyster and I could achieve anything I wanted. Apart from giving me great growth as a professional, this job also played an important role in shaping my life, as this is where I met Andrew.

Andrew Holland came to India as an expatriate in 1997, working for Merrill Lynch Global as their head of research. He had come here to streamline the company's alliance with a local financial company, the DSP Group. Merrill Lynch Global was an important account for us, and it only came my way when my best friend and colleague Sharmin Photographer—who still takes the credit for 'setting' me up with Andrew—handed the account over to me as she was leaving the job. But her handover didn't infuse me with any enthusiasm. 'Beware of this client,' she told me, referring to Andrew. 'He is a tough cookie and he is going to make your life hell.'

While our initial meetings didn't give me that impression, I eventually experienced how tough this cookie was when I had to negotiate with him for rooms his company had booked for New Year's Eve 1999. These rooms weren't for guests or for hosting a party. Instead, these were war rooms set up to fight the elusive Y2K problem that was giving computer-dependant organisations nightmares. Many computer whiz-kids suspected that the upcoming year 2000 would upend the two-digit year format (99 instead of 1999) utilised by early coders (this was done to minimise the use of computer memory, which was quite expensive and not as compact as today). The fear was that the computer would reset to the year 1900 due to a faulty interpretation of the last two zeros in '2000', which would crash computer systems and cause irreversible damage to the stored data.

To combat this impending doom, many organisations had set up backup offices to store their data. One such backup office was being supervised at our hotel by Andrew. This meant I had to negotiate with him on the deals we offered to his company for the rooms. The deal was finally locked for a room at $99, with additional charges for services like laundry and F&B. One evening, Andrew summoned me.

'Sonal, looks like there has been a mistake. I think we agreed on a different deal, which included a discount on additional services.'

'No sir, there's no mistake. The deal was only for a low rate on the rooms,' I replied politely.

My response aggravated Andrew. 'No, that's not right. We had agreed on a discounted rate for laundry and F&B along with this room rate,' he shot back.

Working in hospitality is like walking on a tightrope round the clock. Client servicing is an important part of the job, as it ensures repeat business. So, I tried to push back as gently as possible. I was certain we couldn't offer a discount on additional services at such a low rate. But I didn't have any documentary evidence to prove that to him right then.

'Sir, there has been a misunderstanding. The deal didn't include any other discounts because you asked for a very low room rate.'

The argument kept escalating and Andrew sternly rebuffed every attempt I made to appease him. I felt cornered in front of his colleagues, and the combination of anger and frustration forced tears to my eyes.

Andrew was taken aback when he saw me crying and stepped back immediately, 'Okay, let's take a break for now. We can discuss this later.'

'I am really sorry. I don't know what's gotten into me,' I said to Andrew, apologising for letting my emotions get the better of me.

'No no, don't apologise. I guess we both need to cool off. I'll give you a call later to discuss this. Please take care.' I could see concern in Andrew's eyes, but I didn't want to continue the conversation even for a second longer. Andrew left the room without another word.

Watching him walk away, I felt I had made a huge mistake that could cost us this client. What if he complained to my manager that I couldn't handle work pressure? Could this escalation damage my reputation at work? I spent the rest of my shift dreading a call from my manager to reprimand me. I did receive a call later in the evening, but it wasn't my superior. It was Andrew, apologising profusely, because upon checking his emails, he had realised that I was right about the room rates. Relieved and vindicated, I accepted his apology as humbly as it was possible for me at that moment, but he wasn't convinced that it was wholehearted.

'I didn't like the way you got emotional because of me and I feel very bad about that. If you don't mind, can you just walk across the road to our office and see me in my cabin.'

Andrew's office was in the Tulsiani Chambers on Nariman Point, which was just a stone's throw away from the hotel. All I had to do was cross the road to get there, but I was irked by his request. What kind of apology was this, where I was expected to walk up to his office to receive it? Shouldn't it be the other way round?

But the tendency to serve is drilled hard into you when you work in the hospitality industry. You are taught to maintain a cordial relationship with clients, even if that means walking up to their office so that they can apologise.

However, the apology was worth it. Andrew was truly sorry for his behaviour and wanted me to write off the conversation so that we could start over. 'I would like to make it up to you. Please tell me how can I do that?' he asked sincerely.

Me being me, spoke without putting any thought into my words, 'Buy me dinner.'

I wasn't trying to sound flirtatious. This was a time when women couldn't even openly ask an acquaintance to buy them a drink. Women drinking alcohol raised many eyebrows, even at swanky restaurants. Thankfully, times have changed and women can grab a drink with male colleagues after work without anyone reading too much into it. But back then, for working women like me, having dinner with someone was no big deal—a fun professional transaction with no ulterior motive.

Something shifted between us after this conversation. The dinner was scheduled for a couple of weeks later. We met a few more times for professional reasons before the dinner and, now that the ice was broken between us, I started seeing Andrew in a different light and discovered a softer and more sensitive side to him. I'm sure he felt the same way because, by the time we went for the scheduled dinner, we both knew it was a date. The rest, as they say, is history.

It took some time for our courtship to eventually turn into a lifelong commitment. Andrew was going through a divorce and had two children from his previous marriage. But I was so sure of him that I decided to give our relationship time.

Around this time, Andrew relocated to Malaysia for a two-year stint and he invited me to come with him. 'This is going to be a rollercoaster ride and I have a ticket for you,' he said.

I grabbed the ticket and dived right in, quitting my job and relocating to Malaysia. These two years saw the highs of living with Andrew, a caring partner who showered me with grand comforts. But the low point was not being able to find a job while on a tourist visa, and eventually feeling purposeless, which got the better of me. So I decided to return to India and seek a new career.

I returned to Mumbai in 2001 and started hunting for a job. I tapped into an old Oberoi connection, Mr Sandip Das, who was then the CEO of a telecom company. He instantly connected me with his wife Purnima Das, who was setting up the Indian subsidiary of Kelly Services—the world's fourth-largest recruitment and staffing company. After a conversation with her, I was hired to work in sales at Kelly.

Eventually, Andrew came back to Mumbai in 2002 and we tied the knot in a lavish ceremony held at the Taj Mahal Palace, Mumbai, in 2004.

The best way to describe Andrew is that he is a mix of old-fashioned and modern values and that in a good way. Soft-spoken and a thorough gentleman, Andrew sees himself as a provider, who believes it is his duty to make sure that his family is always taken care of.

But he is also a very progressive husband, who always encourages me in professional endeavours and is mighty proud of my achievements. Despite being immensely successful in his own profession, he is chuffed when someone walks up to him and calls him 'Sonal Holland's husband'. Only a self-assured and secure man can stand behind his spouse happily as she basks in the spotlight, and I feel blessed to have one in my life.

'I couldn't have asked for more ...'
Speech by Sonal's father at her wedding

You know, there are many different emotions I feel today. But the most overwhelming one that I wish to share with all of you is what a wonderful year 2004 has been for us.

At the beginning of this year, we all moved into our new dream home. Both Sonal and Rimal, our younger daughter, took a lot of trouble to make sure it turned out most wonderfully. Soon after, our lovely Rimal was married to Vivek, less our son-in-law and more of a son to us. And now, just a few months after, we gather today to celebrate the marriage of Sonal and Andrew. I could not have asked for more.

Both our daughters are our pride and joy. I recall when I married Rekha, ours was a love marriage, something not so common thirty years ago. When our first daughter Sonal was born, we were filled with happiness. Through the years, we have seen big dreams for her and our expectations of her have always been very high.

I am proud to say that Sonal has not only fulfilled all our expectations but has always strived to surpass them. We taught her to dream big, but she only dreams bigger. She excelled at her studies, is very popular with her friends and always spreads warmth wherever she goes.

What I find most lovable about her is her relationship with us. She is more like our friend and always shares moments of her life with us, no matter how big or small they are. What can I say ... I could go on and on ... But Sonal is just that kind of a unique person. The house will feel really empty without her.

Both Rekha and I are so delighted to welcome Andrew into our family. I have known him through Sonal for a few years now, and all I can say is that it is our honour to have him as our son-in-law. I have seen Sonal and Andrew support each other over the last few years and have absolutely no doubt that they will have a wonderful life ahead. May God bless them with a successful marriage and happiness always.

Most importantly, I wish to sincerely thank all of you for being here today, especially Andrew and Sonal's family and friends who travelled from different countries to grace this auspicious occasion.

Enjoy yourselves. Thank you!

3

'You Should Be Like Her'

By 2006, I had been working for four years as the national head of sales at Kelly Services—a NASDAQ-listed Fortune 500 that was touted to be one of the world's largest staffing companies. My rewarding corporate job had everything an ambitious thirty-something could desire: an impressive salary, the promise of a corner office in a few years, a great rapport with senior leaders of the organisation and a clear path to progress through the ranks. There was one little problem: my job didn't make me happy.

I had been in the same role for six years, and it had stopped challenging me. I had spent the initial years gaining expertise in the corporate world, but eventually, my learning curve had flatlined. There was a kind of mental stagnation that kept me from enjoying my work. Mind you, this can happen to anyone when their job becomes less challenging and there's nothing left to learn. Before I knew it, I was cruising through my work on autopilot.

While the corporate sector pays well, it can erode your individuality. You are limited to being a representative of a large conglomerate, where your actions and opinions are bound by the organisation. Your personality can never outshine the institution you represent. Besides, corporate work can also leave you feeling irrelevant, as your work doesn't impact people's lives. Just ask yourself: if there are two people in a room, one of whom has created a unicorn start-up before turning forty and the other is a top corporate leader with a huge salary, who would you be more drawn to? Whose work will excite you more?

I was the corporate honcho who had nothing exciting to say. There were times when people would approach me at a party, ask me what I did and then stare at me blankly when I told them that I was the national sales head at an HR firm. They didn't know what more to ask me, and there was nothing I could say about my work that would leave them wide-eyed. I was just another senior leader at a large company. I was scared that I would die in anonymity!

I also felt the industry wasn't doing justice to my skill set. While I was great at sales, I wanted to use my talents on a different platform to create a much bigger impact. I wanted my light to shine brighter, and it was clear to me that I wasn't in the right space for that to happen.

Another reason why I wanted to quit my job was to prepare myself for a shift in my personal life. I had been married to Andrew for three years by then and it seemed like the right time to give motherhood a shot. Our marriage had been amazing so far, but working in a nine-to-five job had kept me from enjoying our time together to the fullest. Andrew and I loved to explore new destinations, try different cuisines and have a great time with friends and family. We took at least two vacations every year, and fitting all of that into my leave budget was becoming a problem. I hated missing out on amazing vacations to sit in corporate meetings, mindlessly watching PowerPoint presentations and scrolling through endless spreadsheets. I would rather be sunbathing on a beach in Thailand. My lifestyle surpassed my job, so it made sense to move on and explore what more I could do with my career.

As these thoughts occupied my mind, I felt my focus wavering from work. But I wasn't ready to bid adieu just yet, even though I had mentally checked out of my job. So, I set my eyes on getting the highest employee award that the organisation offered—the Golden Circle Award. This was an annual global award that recognised the best-performing employee in the organisation. I wanted to win this since it would cement my position as one of the company's best employees, not just in India, but all over the world. This goalpost also catered to my need to feel valued for my hard work.

I won the Golden Circle Award in 2006. I was flown to Orlando for a felicitation ceremony that would be attended by more than two hundred senior leaders of the company. It was a moment of great pride for the firm's India arm and my family. Andrew flew to Orlando with me as he wanted to be by my side on my big day.

The organisers had arranged for a bus to pick up all the attendees from the hotel where we had been put up. But when I got ready and came to the hotel lobby, my husband pulled me aside and said, 'You are not going on that bus.'

'How else will I go?' I retorted.

Andrew turned to the hotel's concierge and whispered something to him. Within a minute, a chauffeur-driven luxury stretch limousine cruised through the hotel's driveway and halted in front of us. My colleagues watched in amazement as Andrew took me by the arm and walked me to the car, and the chauffeur held the door open for me. A chilled bottle of champagne awaited as I climbed into the backseat of the limousine.

'You are the star of the evening, so you deserve to be treated like one,' Andrew said as he popped the champagne and poured it into the glasses.

Indeed, I felt like a celebrity, thanks to Andrew! When I stepped out of the car, it felt like I was on a red carpet at the

Oscars. This was truly a memorable night for me and I was elated to receive the award while the top leaders in my organisation cheered for me. Finally, I received the acknowledgement I had been craving for.

On our way back to the hotel, I checked my phone, and it was flooded with messages from friends and colleagues, congratulating me for the award. One particular message formed a knot in my stomach: 'Congratulations Sonal! Looks like you'll be APAC Head in no time,' wrote a senior colleague.

That's when a realisation dawned on me. The award had brought me immense joy and pride, but it didn't excite me. All the thrill I had felt that day was about being recognised for my work and not for what it would mean for my future in the organisation.

My friend was right. I was on track to become the country head or APAC (Asia-Pacific) head in a few years, based on my current career trajectory. But the thought of moving up on the leadership ladder did not entice me. What was the point of climbing this mountain, if I wasn't thrilled by what awaited me at its peak? With the Golden Circle Award, I felt I had achieved the pinnacle of success in this inning of my career, and moving up the corporate ladder could never top the euphoria I felt at this moment.

I woke up the next morning with just one thought in my head—I was done. It was time to resign from this job and move on.

'Andrew, I think it's time for me to quit Kelly Services.'

Andrew wasn't surprised by my decision as he knew I had been struggling to keep my head in the game these past few months. But always the voice of reason, he asked, 'I know things haven't been easy for you lately, but are you sure about this? It will mean putting an end to a career in which you have a promising future.'

'Absolutely. I think I can put my skills to better use than working in a recruitment firm.'

'I know you. If your mind is made up, there's nothing I can do or say to change it. You've already made your decision.'

'There's one thing, Andrew. I know I am meant for something different, but I don't know what that is. I have no idea what I want to do next,' I said.

Andrew reached out to hold my hand and squeezed it tightly. 'Don't worry. Put in your papers and we'll figure something out.'

Knowing Andrew, I was sure my dilemma would constantly play on his mind. Sooner or later, he would help me find a solution to my problem. His assurance gave me the courage I needed to move out of my job. I put in my papers in April 2007 and ended my six-year-long stint in the corporate world. At the age of thirty-three, I was once again unemployed.

Taking time off is very tough for people who are not used to sitting at home twiddling their thumbs. My whole life till that point had been about working hard and hustling my way to the top. Now the phone had stopped ringing, the pile of office-wear in my cupboard got pushed to the back and the days suddenly got longer than they used to be. But there's always a silver lining to even unforeseen circumstances—they can be the jolt that pushes you on an entirely different path and lead you to glory. Even the world's best-known and admired wine—champagne— was invented accidentally.

Let me tell you that story. There was a time when bubble formation in wine was considered a mark of poor winemaking. But then in the late 1400s, temperatures suddenly plunged in the continent of Europe, and the cold temporarily halted fermentation, which is the process by which grape juice is converted into wine. When the temperatures started soaring again in spring, it triggered a secondary fermentation process inside the bottle, releasing carbon dioxide and making the wine fizzy. A taste check made the quality of the vintage obvious.

While winemakers took many more years to perfect the process, that incident is how champagne happened to us. Can you imagine a world without this strange turn of events? A world without champagne, the ultimate symbol of elegance and excellence, would have been a less interesting place to live in. That's why we need to change our outlook towards unanticipated situations. Who knows where they might lead us?

The itch to do something of my own developed soon after I put in my papers. My first thought was to start my own recruitment company. I would dream during the day about building a big business for myself, but by the evening, I would realise that this dream was not for me. This wasn't where my heart lay, and the reason I'd quit my job was that I did not enjoy working in the recruitment industry. My problem wasn't with the employer but with the area of work, and that dynamic wouldn't change even if I started my own recruitment firm.

Next, I thought about opening a restaurant. I could combine my hotel management education with experience in the hospitality sector to launch a venture of my own. But I was more interested in eating at restaurants than running one. The idea just didn't excite me, despite the fact that it played to my strengths, so I decided to drop it. At one point, I thought about taking up another corporate job. But again, I didn't come across an opportunity that was exciting enough to lure me back into the nine-to-five trap.

I felt a gnawing desire to do something different with my career. At that time, India was known as the 'call-centre capital' of the world. I had seen its upward trajectory from being a sunrise industry to becoming a booming one over a short period of time and it forced me to think—what would be India's next sunrise industry? If I could carve a niche in such an industry, it would cement my position as a trailblazer. The idea was to do what had not been done before. Working in a sunrise industry would allow me to place myself uniquely, become a pioneer and thus, have greater earning potential. I was also drawn to the guts and glory that come with working in a new industry where you become a trendsetter.

Despite being restless, I held off on making a hasty decision. For me, this reinvention was like an investment that would pay high gains in the future. I needed to be confident about my next career move.

During this phase, my husband became my anchor, constantly assuring me that we would eventually figure out a way together. Then, one day, Andrew came home carrying an edition of *Financial Times* and gently placed it in front of me, saying, 'You should be like her.'

Now those are dangerous words that no wife wants to hear. You never know what's waiting for you at the end of that sentence. A picture of a reigning Bollywood sweetheart? A French supermodel?

With bated breath, I picked up the newspaper, but I wasn't prepared for what I saw. It was an article about a beverage I drank occasionally and didn't know much about—wine—with the name of its writer, Jancis Robinson MW. She was someone who wrote about wines and enjoyed immense popularity and respect in her field of work, but that meant nothing to me. 'Of all the possible things I could be, why do you want me to be like her?' I asked Andrew, genuinely intrigued. Of the thousands of icons in the world, why had he picked Jancis?

'You know, a couple of days ago I attended a party. There, I met someone from United Breweries and during our conversation, he told me they are planning to go into wine production. That made me think about my days in the UK. When I was growing up, Jancis was educating people about wine in the country. With her books and articles, she made British people enthusiastic about wine. If you had any questions about wine, you knew who would have an answer for you. By earning consumer trust, she established herself at the helm of the wine revolution in the UK. I have been thinking that a similar career trajectory will be very good for you.'

'But Jancis works in the UK and everyone drinks wine there. How will I achieve a similar level of success here in India, where people barely drink wine? Honestly, how many people do we know who love to drink wine and choose it over every other drink?' I asked, perplexed.

'See, that's where you're wrong. Everyone drinks wine in the UK now, but when Jancis started out, England's wine culture was right where India's is today. She catapulted to success because she was at the right place at the right time doing the right thing, and you can do the same here. If you successfully establish yourself as a credible wine expert, as consumer interest in wine grows, your career trajectory will grow alongside that of wine consumption in the country.'

Andrew could see that I was intrigued but not convinced. He knew how to push me in the right direction. 'Take your time and think about it. For starters, why don't you read up about Jancis? You'll see what I mean.'

So, I began reading about Jancis and soon, I understood Andrew's vision for my future. That write-up not only put me on my current trajectory but also introduced me to a woman I've grown to idolise.

Like me, Jancis had a wine-free childhood and adolescence in a village in northern Cumbria, just south of the Scottish border. She was introduced to wine while she was completing her master's in maths and philosophy at the Oxford University. Thus, began her lifelong courtship with wine, which eventually led to her working as an assistant editor with the British wine trade magazine *Wine & Spirit* in 1975. Simultaneously, Jancis started pursuing wine as a subject; she studied it professionally while writing books about it. Then in 1984, she created history by becoming the first person outside of the wine trade to achieve the title of Master of Wine.

For the past several decades, she has been using her authority to produce volumes of books and blogs packed with knowledge about different kinds of wine and varying styles of winemaking, answering every possible question that could cross a person's mind, be it an ordinary consumer or a wine expert. Such is the scale of her contribution to the British wine industry that she was made an OBE (Most Excellent Order of the British Empire awarded by the British monarch) in 2003.

But when Jancis started her career, the UK was not a big wine market. Like India, it was then a non-winemaking country, with minimal interest in the beverage. However, the drive for economic liberalisation in the 1980s saw the proliferation of supermarkets all over the country. Soon enough, these stores could sell wine, and that's when the drink got fully democratised, as it became easily accessible. The consumers didn't have to own wine cellars under their castles to enjoy the beverage. They could walk into a supermarket and buy a bottle while picking up groceries. This ease of purchase and improved accessibility catapulted wine's popularity with the general public. Today, retail trade accounts for nearly 80 per cent of wine sales in the country, with popular supermarket chains like Waitrose, Tesco,

Aldi, Sainsbury, ASDA, etc. commanding the lion's share.[2] While all this was happening, Jancis was right there, leading the wine revolution from the front, teaching consumers the art of enjoying wine and helping wine professionals improve their beverage service and knowledge.

My husband felt I could do something similar in India because, in 2007, India was right where the UK had been when Jancis had started. I asked Andrew why he was so confident that I could succeed in this field. He reasoned that wine required one to have knowledge and be authoritative enough to communicate with confidence. He believed that wine was such a vast and diverse subject that the majority of people would never be able to fully understand it, which was why it would always require someone who knew it thoroughly to take centre stage.

He jokingly added, 'Sonal, being a wine expert will put the spotlight on you, and you'll have a room full of people who would want to listen to you. I know you'll love that.' I let the jibe slide because I knew it was true. The role would indeed play to my strength as a communicator.

'I can imagine you standing on a stage, speaking about wine in front of a large audience and people applauding you. And I also know that you will derive great happiness from it,' he said in a much more serious tone.

I think this idea could have only come from a visionary like Andrew. I had no clarity about what I wanted to do next. Every idea seemed as lucrative as the next one, but I didn't know which one I should bet on. However, Andrew not only had faith in my potential, he envisioned that I would find unprecedented success in the field of wine.

---

[2] 'Spotlight on the UK, a Leading but Highly Challenging Market', *Meininger's International*, 12 January 2023, https://www.meiningers-international.com/wine/markets/spotlight-uk-leading-highly-challenging-market.

I understood his vision, but I needed a target to chase. A footballer can keep running around in circles on a field, but the objective is to score a goal. This is defined by the presence of a goalpost towards which she can run. I needed a similar goalpost so that I knew I was running in the right direction.

'I need to know what I'm aiming for here, Andrew. Otherwise, I'll be running around like a headless chicken.'

'Well, if you need a purpose, why not aim for the highest title in the wine world, the one that Jancis has as well? Why don't you become a Master of Wine?'

I opened my laptop and looked up information about the Master of Wine title. The first thing to pop up was that it was one of the toughest exams in the world, with just 400 or so active MWs holding the title. The second fact that stuck with me, as I read more about it, was that no one from India held the title so far. Did I have it in me to become India's first Master of Wine?

4

New Kid on the Block

Within a few months of quitting my job in 2007, I had chanced upon the nascent Indian wine industry thanks to Andrew, and we were confident that this would be the next sunrise industry in our country. I had to act fast to get the first-mover advantage. However, I barely knew anything about the Indian wine industry. To understand my chances of success, I started following it closely, calling anyone willing to discuss the subject with me.

My research told me that there were just a handful of wine producers in India—Chateau Indage, which is touted to be the first modern winery in India, was on the brink of collapse, and Sula Vineyards was trying to fill this void and use this opportunity to expand. A few producers like Grover Vineyards and Reveilo Wines had been around, growing steadily in popularity. Indian winemakers were setting out to find their brand identity and voice, which could help them connect with a new breed of Indian consumers—young, moneyed and aspirational.

When it came to imported wines, we had some premium French wines like fine expressions from Bordeaux along with some good quality champagne and Châteauneuf-du-Pape from the Rhône Valley available in the country. But wine was barely present in retail stores, and most fine wines were either hand-carried to India by patrons or available through luxury hotels. Until 1990, the import of alcoholic beverages was not freely permitted in India. Only luxury hotel chains, like the Taj and the Oberoi Group of Hotels, were allowed to import liquor and wine for their five-star properties, restricting their availability.

As a result, only senior executives who worked at these luxury hotels in India had access to wine. At the turn of the millennium, when I was still working as a sales executive for Oberoi Hotels, I saw a senior executive at the hotel frequently enjoying a glass of red wine or a scotch with a cigar. The sight of a refined man entertaining his guests after work with wine and cigars was so rare that the image stayed with me. Indian wine-importers often tried to woo general managers of luxury hotels by presenting them with wines from their portfolios on the pretext of sampling and networking after work hours. While they commanded the attention of the early enthusiasts with their knowledge, whatever importers knew about wines was limited to the labels they sold. Furthermore, whatever they knew about these labels was restricted to certain anecdotes or stories and information they had received from the producers.

Mostly, wine-consumption was restricted to the well-heeled, elite communities of Mumbai and Delhi. The consumers were mostly older affluent men, who had worked in influential positions all their lives or had inherited a sophisticated way of living from their families. Despite travelling extensively and being exposed to Western culture, their wine knowledge was limited to name-dropping the most popular styles of wines coming from France and Italy.

'I only drink champagne or red wines from Bordeaux, and occasionally enjoy a Barolo or a Brunello from Italy,' they would flaunt. Who even knows if they were telling the truth! To me, they appeared to be wine snobs who proclaimed to be experts just because they hosted lavish house parties and claimed to drink expensive wines.

There weren't many women who were drinking wine at the time. In general, society was quite conservative and frowned upon women drinking freely. The few who did drink within the upper circles of society would either douse their drink in cola or hide their glasses with tissues when drinking in public places.

Another group of early wine consumers consisted of expats working with embassies and consulates. I remember attending an evening soiree at the home of the trade commissioner attached to the US Consulate in Mumbai a few years after the turn of the millennium. He used to live in a plush apartment at Dhanraj Mahal in Colaba, a stone's throw away from the Gateway of India. He was hosting CEOs, heads of businesses and expats at his home and had proudly poured Californian wines for his guests. We were invited because of my husband's high position in the world of finance. These were the kinds of homes where you would usually find wine served—it was exclusive and elite, not mainstream.

Until the turn of the millennium and for a few years thereafter, wine didn't succeed in grabbing the attention of the average Indian drinker. It was only discussed and appreciated in small circles and there was no knowledge or awareness of it amongst the general public. The reason for this was the absence of qualified wine professionals in the market. Even people who took wine seriously understood very little about it.

If an establishment wanted to hire a wine professional, they would have to recruit someone from overseas. A few experts did move to India and take up jobs as wine consultants in leading hotels. To their credit, they helped hotels list good wines on their bar menus. However, they couldn't change the general perception of Indian consumers about the beverage, as the percentage of drinkers they would interact with was very low.

The five-star hotels where they were employed were well out of the reach of most Indians.

However, I could see some early signs of positive change in the industry, and it seemed to be on the cusp of something bigger and better. It received a boost when the Maharashtra government introduced the Maharashtra Grapes Processing Industry Policy in 2001, which gave impetus to the grape processing and wine industry, and led to the setting up of wine parks in the districts of Sangli and Nashik. The district of Nashik, which was renowned countrywide for its quality table grapes, benefitted greatly from this policy, as wineries and vineyards gradually began to pop up all over the region.

In 2007, Karnataka too introduced its Grape Processing and Wine Policy, under which the grape wine production units were declared as horticulture and food processing industries, thus making them eligible to receive all industry-specific incentives and facilities.[3] One region in the state that was touted to have the right combination of climate and soil for the cultivation of wine grapes was Bengaluru, as a result of which many boutique wineries chose to set up shop in this region. There was another factor working in Bengaluru's favour: the city was known to be the hub of metropolitan culture and had the potential to cultivate a thriving wine scene. Bengaluru had a huge influx of expats and Indian IT professionals who had come back from abroad to work in India's Silicon Valley and brought with them the culture they had experienced overseas. They were not only seeking the wines they had tasted on their travels but also looking to recreate similar experiences, intending to make wine-drinking a part of their lifestyle.

---

[3] 'Karnataka Grape Processing and Wine Policy – 2007', Karnataka Grape & Wine Board, https://wineboard.karnataka.gov.in/info-4/Karnataka+Wine+Policy/en.

Also in 2007, a bureaucratic move triggered a change in the fate of imported wines, by bringing the import duty down from 252 per cent.[4] The catalyst was a complaint filed by the European Union before the World Trade Organization about the aggregate duty level in India. As a result, India eventually slashed import duty on wine to 150 per cent in 2007 to fulfil its obligations towards WTO.

The high import duty on wines was still a grievance for market stakeholders and consumers, but this move showed India's willingness to strengthen its global trade ties. The change in government policies that reduced import duty on international wines and homegrown wine brands in the first decade of the new millennium gave wine new momentum in India. We could see a change in consumers' outlook towards wine in metros like Mumbai and Delhi, as they showed an early interest in the beverage triggered by exposure to Western culture via travel and entertainment.

Importers took the first steps in creating a wine culture in India by organising experiences around wine, such as wine-paired dinners, educational workshops, wine tastings and more. This phase of wine's popularity in India also saw the advent of wine clubs. In Mumbai, expat David Banford started a wine subscription programme called the Wine Society of India in 2006. Born in India, Banford had also run a similar programme in the US, called the Wine Society of America (founded in 1984), which he had sold off before returning to his birthplace.[5]

---

[4] Amiti Sen and Boby Kurian, 'Cheers! Pay less for imported liquor', *The Economic Times*, 21 May 2007, https://economictimes.indiatimes.com/news/economy/foreign-trade/cheers-pay-less-for-imported-liquor/articleshow/2063272.cms?from=mdr.

[5] 'By Invitation Only', Mint, 11 April 2008, https://www.livemint.com/Leisure/lXRlOHdOvKJdQQbu1RYQeJ/By-invitation-only.html.

Banford also brought renowned British wine merchant and expert, Steven Spurrier, onboard as a consultant. Spurrier has a vast legacy of contributions to the field as a merchant, writer and expert, but he is most remembered for organising the famous Judgement of Paris tasting in 1976.[6] This blind tasting was a watershed moment in the history of wines overseas, where wines from California outperformed the finest labels from France. This unbelievable victory consolidated California's position as a producer of superior-quality wines and brought much-deserved respect to the winemakers of that region. This historic event was adapted into a movie called *Bottle Shock* (2008) starring Chris Pine and Bill Pullman, and revered British actor Alan Rickman brought Spurrier's character to life on the silver screen.

The Wine Society of India would send quarterly shipments of selected wines to subscribers, apart from organising meet-ups and educational events once every few months at upscale hotels in cities like Mumbai, Delhi and Bengaluru. The curated wine shipment helped wine lovers bypass the struggle of selecting wines for themselves, while the club's events built wine knowledge from the ground up. You can imagine what a big deal it was for oenophiles in India to receive wine bottles hand-selected for them by someone as distinguished as Spurrier. While the society was popular, it met several regulatory roadblocks and eventually wrapped up its operations. But when it had started, it had been a credible pioneering initiative, perhaps a little ahead of its time.

I could foresee a bright future for wine in India because all the fundamental elements required were falling into place. I was exposed to the UK's wine culture as my husband has family and

---

[6] Jacobo Cristi, 'Judgment of Paris: The tasting that changed wine forever', *CNN*, 24 September 2021, https://edition.cnn.com/travel/article/judgment-of-paris-wine-tasting-cmd/index.html.

friends in Britain and we would visit frequently. We often ended up eating Indian meals as our British friends loved the cuisine, and I would think how wonderful it would be to host a dinner back home with fine wine themed around Indian dishes.

India was also experiencing an economic boom at the time, with a rise in disposable income of its consumers that promised to rouse an aspiration for luxury and all the finer things in life. At that time I felt like I had hit upon a great idea and perhaps I could build a professional career in a new industry that was waiting to explode in the coming years.

I knew one thing—I didn't want to be another cog in the wheel and become a self-proclaimed expert simply by reading a few books or drinking expensive wine. If I was going to do this, I was going to do it right by building my career on a solid foundation of credibility and knowledge. Now this was a cause worth dedicating myself to.

But there were several challenges ahead of me, the first and most important being that I knew nothing about wine. A glass at a party now and then didn't equip me with the knowledge and experience I needed to work in the industry. The second problem was a lack of mentors in India—I had no one who could guide me through the world of wine, and I didn't even know how to find my way myself. Besides, I was plagued with doubts. What was the guarantee that this gamble would work in my favour? What if I was climbing the wrong mountain?

I knew I had to act fast, so Andrew and I sat down to crunch the numbers and see how much it would cost me to become a qualified wine consultant. We were very clear from the start that I must build my wine career on solid credentials. We weren't willing to compromise on my studies, and only the best education that the wine world had to offer would do as that would give me undisputed authority and an edge in the industry.

'Now, we know that if you want to study wines in a proper way, you'll have to do it outside India,' Andrew said to me as we racked our brains to think of all the possible expenses that I could incur.

'I know, but that would mean a lot of additional expenses. I would need a place to stay, I would have to spend on food and I would have to fly out frequently. Then, of course, there will be my tuition fees for all these courses. Wow, this is going to cost a lot!'

'Sonal, it's okay, this is something we have to do. I genuinely believe that you can become a Master of Wine and have a phenomenal career trajectory in this field.'

'But it will take years for that to happen! We don't even know when I'll be able to achieve my goal. It would be better if you invested this money in the stock market. At least you'd be assured of returns.'

'Fair enough. So, we'll look at this as an investment in your future business. I am confident we'll reap rich dividends from it. This will be a long-term investment in your career and I am in no hurry to claim a profit,' Andrew joked. 'No, seriously Sonal, don't think about the money, just go and figure out how to go about your studies.'

Andrew's willingness to invest in me gave me immense confidence. I knew I had a safety net under me in case things went wrong, and that meant I could dare to take up a challenge as tough as the Master of Wine exam. His belief that I could use my education to build a profitable business also gave me a sense of responsibility, as my success could have long-term benefits for us.

The right coach can become your support system and encourage you to take that plunge even if you are not a hundred per cent sure of your capabilities. They are also willing to invest in your future, financially and emotionally, so that you can focus on your goal without worrying about the world. I am so grateful that I found a mentor in my husband and he prompted me to act upon this seemingly outrageous idea.

When we talk about life-changing career moves, we have to acknowledge that they cannot be driven by a singular factor. Your desire to be a pathbreaker isn't enough, neither is your mentor's faith in your abilities nor is confidence in yourself that you are primed for success. My research introducing me to a virgin territory, my exposure to wine culture abroad, a mentor who believed in my skills—all these factors gave me a gameplan and the confidence to execute it.

Now that my mind was made up, I decided to break the news to my parents. My mother, a teetotaller, was not pleased with my decision as she disapproved of me working in the AlcoBev sector.

'What will I tell people when they ask me why has your daughter left such a good job, only to do this instead? And what is this Master of Wine? I don't know what it means, so how will I explain it to our family?'

She couldn't even bear to use the words alcohol or wine, which according to her were one and the same. 'I know you were not happy with your previous job, but can't you do something other than this?' she pleaded.

Her reaction was understandable. You can imagine how overwhelming it must be for a parent to see her daughter quit a well-paying job and choose a career that no one knows anything about.

My father, on the other hand, just asked me one thing. 'What does Andrew have to say about all this?'

'It was his idea, Daddy.'

'Then it is okay, I am sure he must have thought it through.'

When I first introduced Andrew to my father, I had been dating him for just a couple of months and I had decided to quit my job at the Oberoi to go with him to Malaysia. Naturally, my father was miffed at the thought of his young daughter quitting her job to go live with a man in a different country, that too without marrying him. But Andrew managed to win him over in their first meeting. He gave more confidence to my parents about our decision to move in together than I ever could, assuring them that he would take great care of me. The more my father got to know Andrew, the more his trust in his decisions grew, one of which was to marry his headstrong daughter. So once he came to know that pursuing a career in wine was my husband's idea, he was totally on board.

I find it amazing how my father came around to support me even when I was doing something that was outside the scope of his imagination.

When my mother asked me how she was supposed to tell her friends and relatives that I worked in the alcohol industry, my father reasoned with her, 'Rekha, many things in this world are beyond our comprehension. So let's not assume that we know everything or that we are fully exposed to all the possibilities that are out there. Our daughter has seen the world, she socialises with the kind of people you and I have never even met. She has a vision and sees prospects in this field that we can't. As her parents, the best we can do is show faith in her decision and support her in every way possible.'

Only a handful of parents have the humility to accept that sometimes their children know what is best for them. I wish more parents could put faith in their children's decisions, knowing perfectly that times change and so must perspectives.

However, failure to comprehend my new career goal wasn't a generational thing. Even when I told my friends about my decision, it was beyond them. Wine was so new and irrelevant in India at the time that they couldn't see how I would have a good career in this domain.

Not the kind to be disheartened easily, I contacted people from the Indian wine industry to learn more about wine education. We collected information about some of the most reputed wine education institutes in London, but most of them offered weekend wine courses that wouldn't provide me with the sort of command over the subject that I was looking for.

Then, an Indian importer pointed me in the right direction. 'Why don't you check out the website of the Wine & Spirit Education Trust? It's the best wine education institute in the world,' he told me.

'Thanks! I'll do that. Now tell me, what are your thoughts about getting certifications in wine? Do you think it has any career advantages?'

'Oh definitely. These courses are not that popular in India, but it's a completely different story outside India. Everyone, from sommeliers, wine critics and importers to winemakers and retailers, do these certifications. Even those who have an interest in academics do them. Then they go and do a diploma or try their luck with the Master of Wine title.'

'Yes, I've heard a lot about the MW title. Do you think it is worth my time?' I wasn't going to reveal all my cards and tell him that I had already made up my mind to pursue that qualification. But I was curious to know what he thought about it.

'Don't even think about it, Sonal. It will just take so much time and money to go after the title and there is no guarantee that you will even get it. It's next to impossible. Besides, the course is so tough and tedious that you'll be a hundred years old by the time you become an MW, if you ever manage to do so at all,' he said dismissively.

It seemed as if the thought that someone like me could become an MW seemed too farfetched to him.

I had always known that I would be surrounded by naysayers the minute people came to know of my MW pursuit. It was best to keep my plans under wraps for now. I would rather invest my energies in pursuing my dreams rather than trying to convince my detractors to believe in me. Besides, the MW title was far ahead in my journey. First, I needed to find the staircase I would use to climb to the top. I looked up the Wine & Spirit Education Trust (WSET) and realised that I had found my Ivy League.

Like many others, I had assumed that since winemaking is a big business in France, one must go there to learn about it. However, the language of wine is English and, because of that, England has a great proliferation of wine education institutes, out of which WSET stands a mile above the rest. After reading about its courses being globally recognised and endorsed by some of the most eminent wine experts worldwide, it became an obvious pick for me.

I think it is important for me to write about the legacy of WSET to help you understand why I was determined to study there. WSET was founded in 1969 as a charitable trust intended to serve the growing educational needs of the UK wine and spirits industry. This was a time when the UK trade primarily focused on the import, distribution and retail of wine and not its production. At its London location, the WSET initially offered three courses—Certificate in Wines, Spirits and Other Alcoholic Beverages, Higher Certificate in Wines and Spirits, and a Diploma in Wines and Spirits. As recognition for its courses grew, the institute decided to expand to other regions, and by the mid-1990s, its courses were also available in Europe, US, the Middle East and Asia.

Today, WSET courses are available in more than seventy countries across fifteen languages, via a network of over 900 licensed course providers. What's more interesting is that students outside the UK represent over 75 per cent of WSET candidates each year. The institute has broadened its scope and now provides courses in beer and sake too.

It would be fitting to call WSET the Harvard of wine education, as this is the place you go to for a well-structured, benchmark education. It builds up knowledge just as schools do, laying the foundations first and gradually putting the students on track for advanced studies. A student can also pursue the advanced qualification directly if they have experience in the field, a substitute for beginner and intermediate courses.

A student like me, who didn't have a basic understanding of wine, greatly benefitted from the gradual increase in difficulty levels—basics were sorted first before we were overwhelmed with advanced level course materials. People often put together bits and pieces from the vast pool of information on offer when they try to upskill. But I knew such an approach would create shaky ground under my feet, collapsing the day I faced challenges at work. I needed to learn wine systematically, rather than collecting random pieces of information off the internet or doing multiple courses, attending tastings, randomly reading wine books. Pearls of knowledge were everywhere, a certain finesse was needed to string them together into something more valuable, and that's what the WSET courses allowed me to do.

When I enrolled at WSET, I aimed for the institute's flagship diploma course, but I needed to finish some foundational courses to become eligible for it, so I enrolled for the WSET Level 1 and Level 2 Awards in Wines.

The WSET Level 1 Award in Wines is an elementary course which requires students to put in six hours of study time in a classroom with a certified course provider. This is followed by a closed-book examination of forty-five minutes with thirty multiple-choice questions.

The WSET Level 2 Award in Wines is an intermediate-level course that requires students to put in twenty-eight hours of study time, followed by a one-hour-long examination with fifty multiple-choice questions.

Today, WSET courses are available in seventy-four countries across multiple languages like Mandarin, Portuguese, Turkish, Spanish, Italian and so on. Students can also opt for online learning programmes so that they can save on travelling costs and learn from the comfort of their homes without having to compromise on their daily routine or work schedule. But back in 2007, avenues were fairly limited, and going to the institute's flagship school in London was my best bet.

I felt confident that I could clear these two courses back-to-back because I am a quick learner. Another reason why I felt pressed to tackle these two certifications in one go was the cost of travel and stay in London. Staying at a modest hotel near my school for a week was cheaper than flying back and forth.

And so the plan was set and the tickets were purchased. I packed my bags and flew to London. I checked in to a hotel that was a five-minute walk from my school and braced myself for a new start. It is funny how new possibilities can fill you up with excitement and anxiety at the same time. My mind was buzzing with thoughts that ranged from random, contradictory, rose-tinted, cynical to pessimistic. 'This will work out for me,' I thought one second, only to panic the next, thinking, 'Will this work out for me?' Somehow, I managed to settle down and prepare for my first day at school.

In my head, I was going to college in a Karan Johar movie. I expected a large campus with old-world architecture, manicured gardens and grand hallways. But as people find out sooner or later, college life isn't what Bollywood makes it out to be, even when you are going to study at the finest wine school in the world.

Instead, I was greeted by a building on the not-very-glamorous Bermondsey Street that looked, well, very much like an academy. Nothing said wine about this academy—no pictures of wines or grapes on the wall—in fact, there were no wine bottles in sight. The classroom was pristine and sterile, with regular desks and chairs and a whiteboard in front. During the brief orientation, I was given my study kit with a textbook, a tasting manual, a specification booklet and tasting glasses. These were not the magnificent wine glasses we all associate with wine, which have a broad base, an elegant stem and a generous bowl. These were standard ISO glasses that were sturdy yet clear enough to help students observe wines accurately. Just looking at the glasses, I knew that this wasn't a lifestyle course where I would sit and swirl wine stylishly in a crystal wine glass. It was as scholarly as it could get.

Gradually, the classroom began to fill up and I found myself surrounded by all kinds of people from different corners of the world. I was the only Indian, which I found oddly unsettling. We Indians have a strong global presence. Our strength doesn't just lie in sheer numbers but also in our flair to own every street, every city, every position and every workplace that we come to occupy. We know how to make our presence felt. But in that classroom, I was alone and outnumbered and felt disadvantaged. This was unchartered territory, and I was trying to navigate it without a compass.

Once all the students were seated, our educator walked in and asked us to place our glasses in a semi-circle on the tasting mat (a rectangular white sheet usually made of laminated paper). There was no time for introductions, so our teachers jumped straight to relaying instructions, the most disheartening of which was that we were expected to wash our glasses ourselves after every tasting session. While this explained the presence of sinks in the classroom, it deflated my spirits slightly. The thirty-something former director of national sales, the apple of her parents' eyes and the mistress of the Holland household would have to put her airs aside and queue up with other students to scrub glassware. What a bummer! But this was a good reality check for me— education is a great equaliser and also brings humility to our character, as we have to set aside all the pretence and submit to the rules and regulations of the institute, acknowledge the potential of fellow students and follow our teacher's instructions.

The class began and the first slide came on the screen; it simply asked, 'What is wine?'

I had no clue.

Early Years, and Sonal Dives into Wine
Rekha Chandole, Sonal's mother

Women of my generation used to feel that they should have at least one son, especially if they already had a daughter, and I am not an exception. However, my husband was extremely progressive and he would always tell me that our daughters would not only be successful but take care of us in every way possible. His outlook rubbed off on me, and I never felt that something was lacking in our lives because we had two daughters and no sons.

My husband had an extremely jolly nature and he used to get along with everyone, making friends in any room that he would walk into. He encouraged me to work as he felt that when you step out of the house, your world expands and your views change.

I see a lot of his qualities in both our daughters. Both of them are equally intelligent and talented. Sonal is active, ambitious and a visionary like her father. Since there is an age gap of six and a half years between Sonal and her younger sister Rimal, Sonal was the apple of our eyes for a long time. She had such a sweet nature while growing up that it was difficult for us to get angry with her. She had a lot of friends and showed leadership qualities from an early age.

I expected Sonal to help me with household chores once she was old enough as I was a working woman. But my husband would always discourage me, saying that we should let our daughters play, focus on their studies and take part in extracurricular activities instead. When I would argue that they should know how to perform household tasks as well, as that would be useful after they got married, he would simply say, 'They won't have to do any such work. They will have house help.' True to his word, both my daughters have excelled in their careers and have house help to manage their homes.

It was a difficult time for us when Sonal lost her way during her late teen years. No parent likes to see their talented child waste good opportunities. So when Sonal got distracted from her studies, we were extremely concerned.

I used to visit my parents every Sunday, and Sonal's name and antics would inevitably come up in our conversations. I would often complain to my father about her and tell him how she didn't listen to me or barged into my office and demanded money from me in front of my colleagues. Since my parents used to look after Sonal when she was young, they were quite fond of her. So, whenever I complained about her to him, he simply said, 'Why do you worry so much? Your daughter will earn so much money that she'll be able to buy whatever she wants.' While I saw no signs of any such miracle happening back them, his blessings have changed Sonal's life.

Even when we were dejected by how her life was panning out, we never lost faith in Sonal and firmly believed that she would eventually overcome these setbacks, because we knew that our child was extremely intelligent and talented.

We knew of parents who had taken a drastic approach with rebellious daughters, marrying them off as soon as they finished college and putting them on the track to lead ordinary but socially acceptable lives. But we didn't want that for Sonal. We knew that if we continued to be supportive, eventually she would come around, and that's exactly what happened.

When Sonal came to us and said that she wanted to leave her job and switch to a career in wine, I was a bit conflicted about it, although my husband completely trusted her and Andrew's decision. I wasn't uncertain because I didn't trust Sonal, but because this was a new world for me, and a very different one at that too, as wine had never been a part of our lives. I didn't know anything about it. What was I going to say, if someone asked me what my daughter did? How do I explain what a Master of Wine is to a member of the family who, like me, doesn't understand wine?

However, my views have changed over the years and I am extremely proud of my daughter's achievements. I used to always tell Sonal that whatever she touches will turn into gold, and I am happy that she has found a field that does justice to her talent.

I think the one quality that has helped her use her intelligence and skills to become successful is her strong determination. All she has to do is to decide where she wants to channel her energy and after that, she won't stop until she has achieved her goal. This focus is what separates her from other people.

For instance, Sonal's daughter was very young when she enrolled in the Master of Wine programme, but she didn't let that stop her. Besides, she always knew her parents had her back. My husband and I would go to live at her home whenever she was away to take care of Rianna. We always encouraged her to leave the house without a worry in the world so that she could keep her focus on her studies and exams. But we also know that even if she didn't have our support, she would have found a way to make things work.

Sonal's sense of humour and great communication skills make her the life of every party and family gathering. She has a knack for telling stories in such a way that people can't help but get hooked on every word she says. I have seen her behaviour change over the years after getting married and becoming a mother to Rianna. Having a family of her own to care for has made her more sensitive and caring as a daughter.

5

London Calling

While the question 'What is wine?' was as basic as it gets, I was frankly relieved to see it on the screen. This meant that the course assumed students would have zero knowledge of the subject, which is why the journey was starting from the most elementary level possible.

The WSET Level 1 Award in Wines changed how I looked at wine in one day. It began with something as simple (yet highly informative) as understanding the parts of a wine grape, understanding its different styles and how to pair them effectively with food. It was a revelation to find that wine grapes differ from regular table grapes. Primarily coming from the species *Vitis Vinifera*, wine grapes are often smaller and riddled with seeds. They also have a much thicker skin and are sweeter. The sugar in grapes converts to alcohol during fermentation, so the sweeter the grape the higher the wine's ABV (alcohol by volume).

I also learnt that white wines are made using green or yellow grapes. After the grapes are harvested, they are pressed to extract the juice. Yeast is then added to the juice to start the process of fermentation, which lasts for fourteen days. To preserve their delicate flavours, white wines are fermented at lower temperatures than red wines. The wines are then clarified, filtered and bottled.

Red wines, on the other hand, are made from black or purple grapes. Contrary to popular belief, red wine doesn't get its colour from grape juice but from the fruit's skin, which contains a pigment called anthocyanin. After the grapes are harvested, the black or purple grapes are crushed, but the skin and seeds are not separated from the juice. As the grape skins stay in contact with the juice during fermentation, they dye it red, producing that crimson colour that we all love. The skin and seeds also add tannins to red wine, which give it structure and complexity. Afterwards, the skin and seeds are separated and the wines go through clarification and filtration before bottling.

The course introduced me to the main types and styles of wine along with eight principal wine grapes: white varieties like Chardonnay, Sauvignon Blanc, Pinot Grigio and Riesling, and red grape varieties like Cabernet Sauvignon, Merlot, Pinot Noir and Shiraz. While hundreds of grape varieties can be used to make wine, only a handful of them have established a global reputation and are thus known as principal grape varieties. The course also covered topics with practical application, such as how to store and serve wine, principles of food and wine pairing and describing wine using the WSET Level 1 Systematic Approach to Tasting Wine (SAT). The SAT taught students to taste wine in a logical, systematic and professional manner. Our educator tasted nine wines with us to help us understand the process better.

My classes for the WSET Level 2 Award in Wines certification began a couple of days after I completed my Level 1. While the result for the introductory level would come later, I could move up the ladder, as I didn't need to pass the first level to attend classes for the second.

This intermediate course built on my understanding of wine from Level 1. For instance, it covered familiar topics like the eight principal grape varieties along with the style and quality of wines made from twenty-two regionally important grape varieties produced in over seventy global geographical indications (a sign used on products like wine or cheese that have a specific geographical origin and possess qualities or a reputation that are due to that origin). It also elaborated on how grape varieties and winemaking processes influence key styles of sparkling and fortified wines, processes involved in the storage and service of wines and food and wine pairing principles.

The Level 2 course also covered key labelling terms used to indicate origin, style and quality, which tells professionals and consumers about where the wine has come from, and what they can expect from it in terms of taste and quality. Labelling terms are extremely important for European wines from regions like France, Italy and Spain, where a simple mention of the specific vineyard or region will tell you everything about it, from the style and grape variety to tasting notes and even quality. We tasted nearly thirty-five to forty wines using the WSET Level 2 Systematic Approach to Tasting Wine. I passed both courses with distinction.

As soon as I came home after completing Level 2, I began looking for work opportunities that would let me test my skills and newly acquired knowledge. One of my acquaintances told me about a wine programme they had subscribed to. So, I tracked down the organisation that offered this programme and landed in the office of the Wine Society of India at Nariman Point.

I remember walking into the office without any appointment and saying, 'Hi, is anyone here available to speak? I am Sonal Holland and I've just come back from London after doing my Level 1 and 2 in wines from WSET.'

The founders got up from their seats to give me a hearty welcome. They just had one question for me, 'Where have you been all this time?'

David Banford and his partner Kris Engle, the brains behind the subscription-based wine programme of the Wine Society, were well-versed with WSET certification programmes, having lived in the UK. 'We are so happy that someone from India has finally done these courses, congratulations!' David said to me.

'Thank you, David. Now I am looking to try my hand at working in this industry. One of my friends, who is a member of this society, suggested I speak to you. Is there anything I can do here?'

'Your timing couldn't have been better, Sonal! We are looking for someone to conduct workshops and wine-tasting sessions for our members. This will be a freelance job and we will call you as and when the opportunity arises. Is that something you'd be interested in?' he asked.

Of course I said yes, and that's how I got my first stint as a wine communicator. I would be paid ₹15,000–20,000 to host each event, which was insignificant compared to my salary at Kelly Services. But I didn't mind, because I knew that I was working in a new field with only elementary or foundational knowledge, and that I had to build up my career from scratch.

The first workshop I did for the Wine Society of India was held at a plush restaurant in South Mumbai. It was attended by a small group of people who were curious about wine and wanted to learn more about it. I won't lie and say I marched like a lion to the podium. It took some courage to take those first steps towards the mic, but once I got behind it and tapped into my newly gained confidence, there was no stopping me. Even while I was conducting the workshop, I knew I was having a great time, just as my husband had predicted. I could talk for hours about this fascinating subject. It became apparent to me during the workshop that I felt passionate about wine, and communicating about it came naturally to me.

After the seminar, some ladies sitting in the audience caught up with me and complimented me. 'You are really good at this,' one of them said, adding, 'You must be doing this for a long time.'

This was the moment when the penny dropped for me and I realised I was on the right path. This field was no longer just a logical choice; the work was something I enjoyed doing and was great at. As soon as I was sure that wine was the right career for me, I wasted no time and enrolled in the Level 3 Award in Wines course at WSET. Now this was a tougher nut to crack. The challenge with Level 3 is that there is a lot packed into this advanced certification course, because of which students often get intimidated. This certification requires a total of eighty-four hours of study time, including thirty hours of classroom learning and over a hundred wine-tastings.

Level 3 is divided into two units—the first one deals with factors that influence production and the key characteristics of different styles of wine. The unit also discusses how students can apply their understanding to explain wine style and quality. The second unit singularly focuses on tasting wines, describing their characteristics and evaluating their quality, using the WSET Level 3 Systematic Approach to Tasting Wine (SAT).

The examination process adds to the challenge as students have to solve fifty multiple choice questions and submit a short answer paper to clear Unit 1 and blind-taste two wines (one white, one red) without having any knowledge of the producer, the grape variety or the region of origin. Students were required to write an accurate descriptive tasting note for the presented wines using the lexicon of words prescribed by the WSET, identifying their colour, aroma and flavour and textural mouthfeel. The textural mouthfeel includes elements like the wine's sweetness, acidity, body, alcohol level and tannins level (in the case of red wines). For example, a white wine from a cool climate will typically have the aromas of green apples, citrus, lime and pears, whereas one from a warmer climate will display notes of sweeter fruits like mangoes, bananas and peaches. Red wines are known to have aromas and flavours of red-coloured fruits like raspberries, strawberries and plums. Mouthwatering wines are described as 'high acidity' and those red wines with mouth-puckering dryness are said to have 'high tannins'.

The pressure of performing under exam conditions can be intense, especially for those new to the world of wines. While wine tasting can play games with your head, writing the short-answer paper not only tests your English writing skills but also requires you to demonstrate the application of theoretical concepts.

The pressure of transitioning from Level 2 to Level 3 certification was palpable when I arrived in London to attend the classes. I realised that clearing this level wouldn't be a cakewalk and I would have to crank up my efforts by a couple of notches if I wanted to pass this course in one go.

I lived in a small room at a modest but comfortable hotel called Premier Inn. My whole week was spent either at the school or on my hotel room bed, with my textbook and notes spread around me. The only breaks I allowed myself were for meals and tea. Putting in hundred per cent effort when required comes naturally to me; it was like a switch had been flipped and all I thought about for that one week was wine.

My joy knew no bounds when I cleared Level 3 with merit. And when I shared this news with a few of my friends, celebrated journalist and my dear friend Malavika Sangghvi asked me to write a column on wine for the *Bombay Times*. Now, I knew I was good behind a mic, but back then, I simply didn't know anything about writing, and I told her so. But she assured me that she had my back. 'You just write, and I'll edit it for you,' she said.

The article covered the basics of wine and also captured my wine education journey, so that anyone who wanted to study the subject could find guidance through my write-up—something I never had. It was a quarter-page spread for the *Bombay Times'* Sunday edition, and it carried my byline and photograph. Titled *Wines and Roses in Mumbai,* it marked my first tryst with fame. The article is a time capsule that captures Mumbai's blossoming interest in wine and my transition from a sceptic into a wine professional who had found her calling. Here's an excerpt from my first byline to give a glimpse of the days when wine was still on the brink of popularity:

> The Mumbai wine people, as I see them, are waiting to be approached and educated about wines. I mean everybody who is anybody in this city would like to feel less intimidated when ordering wine in a fancy restaurant or selecting a good quality wine for their party. Nobody wants to be a wine nerd anymore!
>
> But let's not kid ourselves. If you enjoy your wine and are looking to gain some structured learning about this wonderful drink, you are more likely to stumble upon a big black hole of nothing. Wine activities, in my opinion, enjoy poor visibility in this city. Tastings and workshops, which are great ways to involve people, are not catching speed. There's not enough wine education being offered in this city ...

It's a different kind of rush, to see your name and picture in a newspaper, to watch your husband and family show off your first media appearance with pride, or to have a long-lost acquaintance call you out of the blue to congratulate you.

The media appearance also felt like a good time to start networking within the wine industry as I had been recently covered in the press, that too with credentials meant to impress.

While I understood wine, I didn't know much about the Indian wine trade. It was important to learn how wine moved around in the industry and found its way to consumers, if I wanted to succeed in the trade. So, I met with leading winemakers, importers and retailers to familiarise myself with the business and to make my presence felt in the industry.

I cannot emphasise enough how important networking is in business. Whether you are a newcomer or a veteran in any industry, it is crucial to be seen. At the start of my career, I would attend all sorts of wine events. These early appearances helped me stand out immediately and brought numerous work opportunities my way. From holding workshops to curating wine lists for popular restaurants in the city, I could see the ball rolling, albeit at a slow pace.

Some of these opportunities paid decently because I dared to ask for what I thought my skills and knowledge were worth, but many others didn't pay at all. I took them nonetheless because I was hungry for work.

My new career was picking up pace, and I wanted to take some time off from my studies to focus on sculpting my profile as a wine professional. However, I reminded myself that it was important to keep my foot on the pedal.

So, after passing my Level 3 exams at the start of 2008, I enrolled in the WSET Diploma in Wines and Spirits course towards the end of the same year. The Institute of Masters of Wine recommends aspirants hold a diploma from WSET or equivalent certification, such as a bachelor's or master's degree in wine (e.g., oenology, viticulture, wine business, etc.) or an appropriate high-level sommelier certificate. The candidates must have worked in the wine trade and have at least three years of professional experience. Studying for my diploma while I built my career would help me hit two birds with one stone and knock off both the prerequisites for the MW programme by the time I completed this qualification. This was the fastest possible route anyone could take to the programme, and I was on it.

I became the first Indian to be accepted into the WSET diploma programme, but I was also aware that my previous strategy to blitz through wine qualifications would not work here. To begin with, the diploma is a two-year programme, and I had opted for a block release course which would require me to fly to London eight times over two years; sometimes to take classes, other times to write my exam. The six essential units covered in the diploma course were designed to develop expertise in a specific area ranging from viticulture and winemaking to understanding different styles of wine. Each unit carried different weightage and required different amounts of guided and private study time.

Students had to taste 220 wines over the two years, all carefully selected to build our analytical tasting skills and contextualise the theoretical knowledge. In total, the certification demanded students to put in 500 hours of study time, including 125 hours of classroom-based learning.

During the diploma course, I got to explore London and make new friends who opened a whole new world for me, showing me around the city and introducing me to new bars, restaurants and to the ever-evolving wine culture of the city. They also took me shopping. Suddenly, I was exposed to international brands; not high-end couture that was way too expensive, but prêt lines that were worn by people in their day-to-day lives. I used to wear shirts and pants or sarees till that point in my professional life. But now I was excited to experiment with new styles of clothing. I realised A-line dresses suited my body type and I started loving scarves so much that I bought a dozen of them. And let me not get started on my penchant for shoes and bags!

This reinvention was my way of becoming a part of the crowd around me. I wanted to look like a wine professional. I would seem approachable and also command respect this way. Many people might disagree with this thought process, arguing that you shouldn't have to change how you look to be accepted in a room full of professionals. But every leader will tell you this— you have to look the part to play the part. There is a reason why entrepreneurs and corporate leaders pay close attention to their appearance, as what you wear can instil confidence in you and those who work for or with you.

When I started working at twenty-five, I didn't know where my career was headed. But I ensured I took up every opportunity that came my way and eventually, showed the courage to leave it when things were not working out.

Today, people typically want to know their passion and purpose in life upfront. But that's not how it works. You have to try your hand at a hundred different things to find your calling in life. This task demands years of patience and resilience before the path shows itself. In this journey, you will climb several wrong mountains, but no one can hand you a map and point you to the right one—you'll have to find it yourself. Some will continue climbing the wrong mountain because they don't want to lose all the time, resources and effort they have invested in the first place. Then there will be those who will be demoralised by repeated failure and stop looking for the right mountain altogether. Only a few will have the tenacity to pursue their calling despite multiple setbacks, and eventually, it will pay off.

Sonal Endears Herself to Everyone She Meets
Chris Holland, Sonal's stepson

I met Sonal when I was twelve. My sister and I flew to Goa for a family holiday, and even though I was meeting her for the first time, we hit it off immediately. Not only did she have a great personality, but she matched my energy. We have always been close ever since, but over the years, we have grown closer as she has evolved in her professional life. She's the first person I reach out to if I need to change certain aspects of my personal or professional life. The best thing about her is that Sonal has a knack for endearing herself to everyone she meets. She always ensures that the person she is talking to feels cared for.

Sonal has done more than she had expected to in her wine career. Her success is an inspiration to a lot of people, especially me, since I'm equally passionate about entrepreneurship. It's amazing when my friends tell me that they are following her on Instagram and they find her work inspiring. She's taking massive advantage of what she's been able to achieve.

Sonal's Reinvention of Herself
Charlotte Holland, Sonal's stepdaughter

I have seen Sonal transform over the years. Today she seems so confident and happy, and I truly admire how powerful she is in her area of work. People appreciate her for what she does and whenever we step out, we will run into someone who knows her or follows her on social media. It takes a lot of courage to change your career at a certain age and not care about what people will think. Her journey has inspired me to reinvent myself because if Sonal can do it, so can I.

I am moving to Australia from the UK in my thirties for a fresh start, and not many people have been supportive of this decision. Sonal, on the other hand, has shown complete trust in my judgement and has encouraged me to fearlessly try different things till I find something that works for me. A few months ago, I met her in the UK, and we talked about how I was in two minds about making this life-changing decision. She asked me where I was on a scale of one to ten in terms of happiness. When I said three, Sonal asked, 'Is there anything that can bring this score up to seven or eight?' I said going to Sydney and starting all over again would do that. 'Then don't think about it too much, just go,' she said without hesitation.

Ever since, I have had many long conversations with Sonal about reinventing myself and giving my career a new direction. I can always count on her for great career advice.

6

She's Definitely Mine

The journey to reinvent myself extended beyond my appearance and enveloped my personal life in 2009, that too in the sweetest way possible.

Andrew and I had been trying to conceive for the past five years. I had developed severe medical issues which made natural conception difficult. I had already been through three to four surgeries for fibroid removal, and we had attempted five to six rounds of IVF, but to no avail.

I became so desperate to have a baby that I tried every possible remedy from naturopathy and ayurveda to astrology and numerology. Nothing seemed to work, and I felt like every door was closing on me.

At this time, three things happened. Andrew had once said, even before we got married, that he would love to adopt a child. I had forgotten about this conversation while I was struggling to conceive. All those years later, I remembered it, and we spoke about it again. Andrew was still for it, but I wasn't yet sure, so I immediately called my mother to sound her out.

'Mummy, Andrew and I are thinking of adopting a baby. What do you think?' I asked, a little hesitant.

'That's a great idea, Sonal!' came my mother's immediate reply. I was taken aback at how promptly she had accepted the idea, while I was still apprehensive. 'Are you sure? I don't want to rush into anything I am not prepared for. What if ... I can't connect with the baby?'

'Sonal, I know one thing for sure, you will be the best mom a child could ever ask for. Adoption is a great option for you, and we'll make sure that the child receives all the love and care that we can give him or her. And I believe God will bless you with a beautiful baby that has come into this world just for you and Andrew.'

This was the second affirmation I received. The third one came from my best friend Sharmin, who simply said, 'Just go for it, babe. Don't even think about it.'

That very moment, a door opened and changed my life forever. I was speaking with an industry colleague who told me about this amazing place, from where she had planned to adopt a child when she had been facing fertility issues too. However, as luck would have it, she got pregnant and put her adoption plan on hold as she felt she wasn't equipped to care for two young children. My friend felt guilty about having cancelled the adoption, and she wanted to complete the circle by helping someone else do the same. She helped me make an appointment at this place. The second I stepped into the adoption home, I knew I was going to be a mother soon. It had a wonderful aura, full of love, kindness and blessings, and I could feel it enveloping me.

Adoption can be a gruelling process for a lot of people. I have heard of incidents where it has taken years for the endless formalities to be completed. But somehow, things just fell into place quickly for us. I think the universe was making up for all the times it had denied me motherhood. We ticked all the boxes of eligibility for prospective parents, our home survey went well, and I assured the adoption agency that this was the only child I would ever have and I would ensure that they got the best possible upbringing.

While gender was never a criterion for us while adopting, my husband secretly wanted a daughter, and miraculously, within two months, all the prayers and wishes that we had ever had over the years were answered. We got a call from the adoption centre saying that our baby was with them. 'You know, she looks just like you; she has your rosy, plump cheeks,' the person from the agency said.

'She has ... you mean it's a girl?' I remember asking.

'Yes, I get a feeling that you wanted a daughter.'

We did, indeed.

'So, when are you coming to see her?'

Meeting my daughter for the first time was a surreal experience. I had been waiting for this moment for so long, but when it came, it felt like I was in a fairy tale. All I remember from the ride to the centre is an unbearable mix of joy, anxiety and excitement. I prayed for the strength to love the child placed in my arms without inhibition. The biggest apprehension before adoption that any parent has is about being able to connect with the child instantly and instinctively. Parents often look at their children and try to find a bit of themselves in them. It could be the appearance, the mannerisms or a quirky habit that brings in some resemblance. In cases of adoption, you know these things are not going to be there, and being a first-time parent, I didn't know whether or not I would be able to overcome that.

Finally, I got to meet her. A care provider put her in my arms and I just went blank. I kept staring at her—she was so beautiful. My husband pleaded with me to let him hold her too. Then something magical happened; as soon as Andrew took her in his arms, she gave him a big, broad smile. 'She's definitely mine!' Andrew exclaimed.

Years ago, when I was still dating Andrew, we'd had one of those cheesy conversations where couples think about the names of their future kids. I told him that I had this name in mind—Rianna—and that I was in love with that name. Andrew, on the other hand, said that if he ever had a daughter with me, he would like to name her Rachel. So, we decided that day that we would name our future daughter Rianna Rachel Holland.

During this visit to the adoption centre, I called my astrologer to give him my daughter's date and time of birth so that he could draw out her horoscope. I told him I needed to know everything he could come up with in ten minutes. He did come through and told us that my daughter had a great destiny and that her name should start with the letter 'R'. That was the moment I knew she was my Rianna. The connection I made with her in that moment was so instant, so permanent, so unconditional and so absolute that nothing in the world could challenge it. When I picked her up again, I observed that she had a mole on her arm, just like my father, and at the exact same spot! She shared something with the man who had always held my hand and encouraged me to become the best version of myself. I was sure my daughter was about to do the same.

It was heartbreaking to leave her behind as the process of adoption was ongoing, and prospective parents were not allowed to take newborn babies home with them till it was over. We had to complete many legal formalities to ensure that the adoption went uncontested. The months leading up to the day we could bring our baby home felt like an eternity, but it finally came! When we went to pick up Rianna, we were led by a care provider into a large nursery, with rows upon rows of tiny humans lying in cribs, waiting to be taken home by doting parents. The nurse playfully said, 'Let's see if you can find your daughter.'

Now, there are a few things about babies I learnt that day—first, they all look very similar. There's a reason why they put a tag around a newborn's ankle at the hospital, because even God, let alone doctors and nurses, would have a hard time telling one baby apart from another in a sea of scrunched-up faces. I started peering down each crib to see if I could identify Rianna. However, one particular newborn didn't approve of this invasion of their privacy and objected quite vociferously.

And then I got my second lesson—if one baby starts crying, every baby in the room begins to bawl too. Soon, I was standing in a room full of crying babies, no closer to identifying my child. But then, one of the crying babies lifted her hand to rub her teary eyes in quite a dramatic fashion and I saw the mole on her arm. There she was! The nurse was impressed with me but I knew it was my dad who had found a way to come to my rescue in the cutest way possible.

My family had planned a huge welcome for my daughter at home. They had covered the corridor to my house with rose petals, and my mom was waiting at the door with a platter for the aarti. I couldn't wait to introduce Rianna to her family, one that was going to shower her with love every day.

The journey we undertook to bring Rianna home allowed us to be together as a family for the first time. I remember driving from the airport with Rianna sleeping peacefully in my arms. We were crossing the Worli Sea Face, and the rays from the setting sun gave an angelic glow to her little face. Suddenly, my heart skipped a beat and I realised that from this day on, I was always going to be a mom. You can undo a marriage or a friendship; you can change careers or reinvent your appearance. You can change every aspect of your life, but motherhood is permanent. Once you become a mom, you always stay one. I had been trying to have a child for so long; it had finally happened and it couldn't be undone.

While this feeling was both comforting and reassuring, it also left me with a huge sense of responsibility. I had to set a great example for this little girl, not only as a mother but as a woman. I wanted my daughter to believe from an early age that a woman can do anything she sets her mind to. At that moment, I was determined more than ever to become a Master of Wine. However, I knew that that wouldn't be enough. I wanted to teach Rianna that every achiever must take it upon themselves to give back to society for the greater good. If I wanted to lead by example, I had to find a way to do that.

The first three months after we brought Rianna home passed by in the blink of an eye, and I couldn't have enough of her. Life felt complete for the first time, and I wanted to stay in this moment for as long as I could. But the clock was ticking, and I needed to return to my studies.

I had embarked on this professional journey because I had bet on the growth of the Indian wine industry. I had hoped that like me, more people would eventually enter the wine sector and help it flourish. However, this industry couldn't grow and gain any momentum without the availability of world-class wine education in the country. Access to quality wine education via globally recognised courses was the only way we could create a cadre of qualified wine professionals whose skills matched international standards.

Parallelly, I was immensely inspired by my learning curve at WSET and couldn't help but marvel at their course structure, which made learning a gradual process that yielded long-term results. I liked the professionalism with which these courses were taught, how WSET had designed its syllabus to meet different requirements and how they had scaled and expanded the institute to establish a presence across numerous countries.

It quickly occurred to me that I could perhaps bring their courses to India by applying for a licence to become an Approved Programme Provider (APP). So, on one of my trips to attend a session for my block release diploma course, I paid a visit to the school's administration office.

'Hi, I am Sonal Holland. I am a DipWSET student at the institute and I have a question for you—can someone from India apply for the APP licence?'

'Of course, they can.'

'Okay, so I want to get an APP licence. What do I need to do?' I asked, hoping for a process that wouldn't take years, or even months, to complete.

'You have to fill out an application form. After that, the institute will verify your credentials. You'll have to go through our Educator Training Programme to teach our courses. Once you complete these formalities, you're good to go.'

The constant feeling of racing against time had put my mind and spirits in top gear. I wanted to have a first-mover advantage in India's wine education sector. So, instead of waiting to finish my diploma course, I signed up for the Educator Training Programme and applied for the APP licence. I knew I was piling on more studies on an already packed schedule, but if I missed this opportunity, someone else would take it up and gain an enviable lead in the industry.

Before launching the academy, I had to find an appropriate name for it. I was in this for the long haul, so my vision was to build an asset that strengthened my legacy with each passing year and was held in high regard by industry and consumers alike. I wanted my vision and aspiration to reflect in the academy's name.

Initially, I thought of naming it the Indian Institute of Wine Education, but it sounded too generic and stood the risk of getting lost in the crowd, once wine education flourished in India and several other institutes opened. Eventually, it dawned on me that for the academy to carry my legacy, it had to be named after me.

Besides, in the world of wine, knowledge is often associated with the name of the person who carries it. For example, Robert Parker's name is associated with the 100-point scale for rating wine, which revolutionised how people perceived and picked wines. Your personal credibility draws people who want to learn more about a subject like wine which is a highly specialised subject. Since I had made up my mind to become the voice of wine in this country, it was only appropriate to name the institute the Sonal Holland Academy.

I wanted the academy to be asset-light to improve its chances of survival and success. Thus, this was to be a virtual academy that could operate out of any premises with a licence to serve liquor. I would approach hotels and restaurants with a proposal to conduct WSET certifications for their staff or to hold regular sessions for wine professionals and consumers. This would allow me to teach at their restaurants or banquet halls using their resources, such as wine glasses, wine bottle openers, wine chillers, projectors, mics, televisions, speakers, etc., instead of purchasing them.

Many APPs around the world operate on a similar model to cut down on the cost of setting up a physical premise and maintaining it. A wine academy is an expensive asset to manage, especially since batches aren't conducted daily, like in management or science colleges. It wasn't until 2023 that I was finally able to set up a physical academy in Worli, Mumbai. Many wine academies, however, choose to remain asset-free forever.

Once the exciting phase of setting up a wine academy was over, things slowed down considerably, much to my surprise. To me, the academy was a superb idea and I expected it to take off immediately. I had envisioned a queue of eager students signing up for the courses, excited to learn about wine. But no such thing happened.

I reached out to hotel general managers and offered courses for their staff, but they deemed them unnecessary, some writing it off as an extra cost. So while I had set up the academy because I'd sensed a gap in the market, I soon realised that there was no market in the first place. I had to create the market first, by popularising wine and conveying the need for qualified professionals in the wine industry.

So far I had only thought about the advantages of being a pioneer in the industry. But the challenging aspect was that I would have to build a market by going door to door and explaining to people why they needed to plan for the future and invest in my vision. To do this, I would reach out to leaders in the hospitality industry and tell them that while training their staff may not directly generate revenue today, it would pay off in the future. There was data to prove this too. They would ask me for the data, but sadly, I didn't have any India-specific data to present. With no benchmark or reference point, it was hard for the academy to gain momentum. But I never gave up and continued with my studies.

In 2010, I became the first Indian to earn a Diploma in Wines and Spirits from WSET. I continued to grow as a professional, patiently waiting for someone to show faith in my vision for the academy. It would have been easy to shut it down and move on, but I didn't give up because I knew I was just a bend away from hitting gold.

In 2024, I attended Ed Sheeran's concert in India, during which he recalled how he got his first hit 'A Team':

When I was eighteen years old, I was playing in pubs in London. I was doing open mic nights. And these open mic nights, when I say I was playing them, it was usually to empty rooms or to people with their backs to me who were not there to watch music. But every week you [Sheeran] would go in with a different song and every week you think that would be the one that changed it all, and every week, you were proved wrong. I wrote this song and I thought this was a special song, and I went in to play it an open mic night. In my mind I was like, this is the song that's gonna change everything and I played it and no one cared. So I went back the week after and I played it again and no one cared. But I believed in this song and I thought this was a good song. So I went back again and I kept playing it again and again to these empty rooms. And then sometimes, people would turn up to hear the song. Then after a while, a lot of people would turn up to hear the songs. And then after a while this song became a minor hit in the United Kingdom and then I signed a record deal and then it became a big hit in the UK. And then that opened up doors into Europe, South America, America and Canada and I remember the first time being asked whether I wanted to come to Mumbai in India in 2015. At the time, never having visited India and always having admired it from afar for the culture and coming here and being so grateful that this song had opened up the door for me to be able to stand on the stage and sing for you.[7]

I have heard many other leaders echo this sentiment that just because an idea doesn't make money or take off immediately, it doesn't mean it's not worth pursuing. 'When something is important enough, you do it even if the odds are not in your favour,' Elon Musk said in an interview when he was asked why he chose to venture into manufacturing rockets and spacecraft despite not knowing anything about them or about how they

[7] Instagram Reel posted by @sonalholland_masterofwine, 17 March 2024, https://www.instagram.com/reel/C4mfrAsPEyr/?igsh=NXZ6bWQyamVnZWZo.

are built.[8] So strong was his belief that he turned the tide and found success.

If you believe in an idea and know it makes sense, you should not give up on it, even if others cannot see its potential. I wouldn't lie and say this conviction came effortlessly to me. At times, I was fed up and felt like giving up on the academy. There were other, more lucrative things on the horizon for me and I was confident my credentials would help establish me in the wine industry. But the academy was so close to my heart that I couldn't bring myself to hang up my boots. I was the most qualified wine professional in the country even then. If I didn't push the envelope for wine education and explain to the world how it bettered prospects for the industry, who else would?

So despite the disappointing results and negative responses from the hospitality and beverage industry, I never gave up on the academy because I truly believed in the idea.

[8] 'When Something Is Important Enough, You Do It, Even If The Odds Are Not In Your Favor - Elon Musk', M3 Motivation, YouTube, 3 April 2021, https://www.youtube.com/watch?v=ViOdlRzq3MY.

A Daughter's Opinion
Rianna, Sonal and Andrew's daughter

Mum always looks out for everyone around her, especially if they are going through a rough time. Another thing I admire about her is how ambitious and hard-working she is, although I wish I could change how much she works so that she has more time for her friends and family. Whenever we are in the car, she's talking on the phone, or when we are on holiday, she's always doing work.

Another thing I would change about her is how much she cares about her hair. For example, we were in the Maldives and she wouldn't go into the ocean or pool until the last day because it would ruin her hair. We were in the Maldives, where the only thing to do is swim in the ocean!

One of the best moments I've shared with her is when I convinced her that we should get a dog. Two days later, I got to take a half day off from school and both of us went to a vet and picked up my companion Ollie. It's been the best two years with him and it was all because of my mum, because, trust me, my dad was not convinced about getting a dog.

Mum isn't strict at all, except for my studies, but only for my tenth grade, as it is an important year and the IGCSE exams are a big deal. But overall, no she's not strict.

7

If Not Me, Then Who?

I wanted to take a break after completing my diploma to focus on building the academy and enjoying Rianna's childhood. But Mr Holland disapproved of my plan.

'The chance to become India's first MW is a once-in-a-lifetime opportunity. What if someone gets the title before you? You should apply for the programme immediately.'

As Andrew predicted, two other Indians applied to the IMW around the same time as me. Had I taken a break before or during the MW, either of these people could have easily overtaken me. As it happens, neither candidate eventually earned the title, but at that moment, just the possibility of other Indian contenders was enough to get my adrenalin pumping, and I sprang into action. It was time to begin the toughest journey of my life.

To enrol in the MW programme, a candidate must submit a letter of reference from a Master of Wine or a senior wine trade professional. This serves as an endorsement of your potential and has to be compelling enough to convince IMW that you have what it takes to earn the title. This is where gaining goodwill in the industry through relentless networking comes into play. For people born within the wine community, with winemaker parents, trade-expert uncles or lineages that can be traced back to vineyard owners, this is just part of the process, as they inherit prominent industry connections that can be tapped into as and when needed. However, for an outsider like me, it meant putting in years of hard work to build this network from ground zero.

By 2010, when I applied for the MW programme, I had developed significant connections in the wine industry and even got a beautiful reference from the very well-known Steven Spurrier, who had witnessed my work for the Wine Society of India, the community that offered me my break in the wine industry. Spurrier had seen me evolve from a starry-eyed new kid on the block to India's most qualified wine expert with a WSET Diploma, who wanted to put her country on the global wine map. He truly believed that I had it in me to realise this dream.

I got accepted into the programme, which is divided into three stages. Stage one or the foundation stage ends with an assessment exam in London, Napa or Adelaide. It involves one twelve-wine blind-tasting paper and the writing of two theory essays. Think of it as a preliminary exam, as you can't advance to the second stage unless you clear it. Quite a number of students don't make it past this stage and are asked to re-apply. The next best outcome is being told to proceed with caution and lots more preparation. The most prepared students get a clear pass to the next stage.

The second stage is the main exam and consists of two parts—the theory and the practical exam. The theory exam is a closed-book written exam—four papers (now expanded to five papers) over a span of four days, whilst the practical exam involves blind-tasting thirty-six wines over three days. All the exams test a student's ability to demonstrate an in-depth understanding of a broad range of wine subjects, as well as accurately taste, assess and draw conclusions about the quality, origin, grape variety, winemaking techniques, commercial potential and other relevant attributes about wines from around the world. Students need to be able to communicate knowledge effectively in writing in a tightly time-controlled environment and demonstrate critical analysis and originality of thought, supported by relevant examples from around the world.

Only after passing the theory and practical components of the MW exam, candidates move to stage 3 of the study programme, the submission of a research paper—an open-book, research-based essay, consisting of 6,000–10,000 words of original writing involving in-depth study and analysis in an area of the student's choice.

On successfully clearing all three stages of the programme, you get admission to the membership of the IMW, after signing an overarching code of conduct.

Stage 1 of the programme began with a five-day residential induction session held in Rust, Austria, a region known for its sweet wines. The induction seminar always takes place in February, and the biting cold weather only added to the chills I felt in my spine, building up to my first rendezvous with the programme. So far, I had breezed through all my exams and was feeling extremely confident of my abilities. How wrong I was!

When I walked into the classroom, I saw twelve identical glasses of wine and a blank paper placed on each of the students' tables. Our instructor cut short the pleasantries when he walked in and asked us to taste the wines and write down our observations like an MW. Did I hear him right? Had I come this far from home, in clothes clearly not suited for the numbing weather, to take an impromptu wine-tasting test at par with MW standards?

We were given two hours to write the paper, and the minute we were asked to start, there was a deafening silence in the room, with all heads buried deep in the paper. All, except mine. I knew how to taste wines, but the questions were different from the kind that I was used to. So I panicked and lost my sense of smell and taste along with my ability to string a sentence together. At this point, I seriously just wanted to run home. Somehow, I pulled myself together and managed to scribble a few lines, hoping to scrape through.

Once everyone was finished, the instructor randomly called on students to read their answers aloud. I was certainly not prepared to read mine and prayed that he wouldn't choose me.

The next thirty minutes were torturous. Qualified people from all over the world fumbled, getting answer after answer wrong.

While we were being subjected to this preview of how miserable our lives would be in the coming years, the head of examinations for the IMW walked into the room and casually dropped a dire prophecy—only four amongst those present in the room would become MWs. I looked around—there were over a hundred people around me. Again, I was the only Indian in the room. Some students came from reputed families that had produced wines for generations, others had decades of experience working in the industry. And here I was, probably the least experienced person in the batch, with no background in wine and no legacy to my credit. How dare I even dream of becoming an MW?

At that moment, I had to rely on the confidence and inner strength my parents had instilled in me since childhood, with their constant belief in my capabilities. 'There's nothing you cannot do, Sonal. You are such an intelligent girl. If not you, then who?' my mother would always say.

I reminded myself that I was here for a reason and that this was my destiny. Had I not said this to myself, I would have cracked and given up soon because the pressure was too much. I had to believe that no one was more capable of achieving this feat than I was. That kept me from quitting, despite days of writing imperfect answers, being unable to correctly identify the wines presented for tasting and running the risk of making a complete fool of myself in front of my peers and counsellors.

I still remember the day I made a terrible mistake during one of the tasting sessions, which taught me an important lesson. We had just finished tasting twelve white wines and were asked to identify the grape variety, the origin and the quality of the wines. The session was being conducted by an MW.

As soon as we finished writing, he went around the room, asking students to read their answers. 'Alright, Sonal, please read your answer for Wine no. 3,' he said.

I knew I was in trouble right away because I wasn't confident about this particular wine. I fumbled through a few lines of weak arguments to deduce that Wine no. 3 was a Viura from the Rioja region of Spain and was a wine of average quality. As soon as those words were out of my mouth, I knew I had made the worst blunder of my life. The entire room went silent and I could feel everyone looking at me in disbelief.

'That's an interesting choice, Sonal, thank you for reading out your answer. Why did you pick Viura?'

'Well, the golden colour, the aromas of peaches and tangerines, the high acidity and the distinctive notes of coconut from oak ageing led me to Viura.'

'Good logic, Sonal. But why can't this be a Chardonnay from Burgundy?'

I had no answer. I knew I had screwed up.

The thing was, even I hadn't been convinced of my answer but I had tried to shoehorn the wine, rushing to make a conclusion without carefully considering all my choices. At some point while tasting the wine, my mind had decided that it was a Viura from Rioja, and then it picked up other clues to confirm the same conclusion. This was the worst mistake a student could make in a tasting—pre-emptively deciding what the wine was and then finding clues to justify the choice. Once you go down this slippery slope, you end up finding notes of oak ageing in a wine where there aren't any, and you feel the wine has high acidity, when, in fact, it might have low levels of acidity.

'I would like to say this out loud to everyone in the room— the one thing that you all must have a great command over are the classics. No matter what, you must be able to recognise the classic wines in your exams and write a strong-tasting note for it,' the instructor said without singling me out.

The classics are benchmark styles of wine that are revered for their elegant and iconic taste. Some classic wines that all wine connoisseurs hold in high regard are the white Burgundy, red Bordeaux, Australian Shiraz, Californian Zinfandel, Champagne, Napa Valley's Cabernet Sauvignon, Argentinian Malbec, among others. A student is not expected to get all the wines right during the MW exam, but a good command over identifying the classics does demonstrate your knowledge and expertise in tasting.

The wine in my glass that day was Puligny-Montrachet—a super-premium white wine from the Burgundy region of France made from the Chardonnay grape variety. Once I knew what it was and had tasted it again, I could see exactly why it wasn't a Viura but a Puligny-Montrachet. I learnt an important lesson that day—keep your confirmation bias aside while tasting a wine, else results could cost you a precious year. I promised myself that I wouldn't let this happen again.

During lunch, one of my fellow MW aspirants came over to chat.

'I looked like a real fool, didn't I?' I said, dejected.

'Of course not!' he exclaimed. 'Do you really think everybody else got all their answers right? No. We're all learning. We're all getting our wines wrong. Don't let this dishearten you. We are all in this together.'

His words encouraged me, and it dawned on me that the course was a great equaliser. The programme may seem like something meant for a bunch of wine elitists flaunting their knowledge, but in reality, it is not. We were all equal in the classroom, failing together, yet not losing the hope to achieve the title. We were all empathetic towards each other and accepted that we were like any other student on the course, none of us smart enough to know it all. The course was bound to be dotted with more failures than successes as we were likely to get more wines wrong than we ever got right in the process of mastering this subject. This realisation was even more humbling for people coming with impressive work experiences or illustrious backgrounds.

Before I tell you what lies ahead, let me brief you on the relevance of the IMW in the wine world. The IMW is a membership-only organisation whose members are Masters of Wine. The IMW's mission is to promote excellence, interaction and learning across all sectors of the global wine community. MWs prove their understanding of all aspects of wine by passing the MW exam, recognised globally for its rigour and exacting standards. After passing the exam, they are entitled to use the initials MW with their names. Since the inception of IMW and its first exam in 1953, only 516 people have become MWs, and currently, there are a little over 400 active MWs across thirty countries.

The institute traces its origin back to two companies; the Wine and Spirit Association, which represents over 300 companies that produce, import, export, transport and sell wines and spirits in the United Kingdom and the Vintners' Company, known as the spiritual home of international wine trade that has a strong association with the import, regulation and sale of wine in the City of London.

These two formidable associations had felt that there was a need to improve the standards of education in the British wine trade while formally certifying its most talented members. So, the first MW exam was organised in 1953 with twenty-one participants, out of which only six passed and became the world's first Masters of Wine. In 1955, the first six MWs in the world—Reg Barrett MW, Leonard Dennis MW, Geoffrey Jameson MW, Rob Kewley MW, Geoffrey Nobes MW and Kenneth Simonds MW—established the IMW.

While the IMW has always been open to women, it took fifteen more years for the world to get its first woman MW, Sarah Morphew Stephen MW (women make up more than a third of the MWs in the world today). However, several barriers still remained, as for a long time, the title was awarded within the British wine trade only to retailers, merchants etc. Then in the 1980s, the IMW opened its doors to applicants from outside the wine trade such as sommeliers, wine critics, winemakers, educators and others. That's how Jancis Robinson MW became the first 'non-trade' person to become an MW in 1984. Another important breakthrough came in 1988, when Australia's Michael Hill Smith MW became the first person to receive the certification after the institute started accepting applications from outside of the UK. It took twenty more years for the title to reach Asia; in 2008, Hong Kong's Jeannie Cho Lee MW and Debra Meiburg MW along with Singapore's Lisa Perrotti-Brown MW brought glory to the Asian continent.

Contrary to what many believe, the MW is a qualification and not an academic degree. It is best suited for people working in the international wine trade, such as winemakers, wine critics, writers, sommeliers and importers, who can further the scope of wine across the world by contributing to different spheres in the industry. Since the MW study programme is now pursued internationally by students across forty countries, the exam is now held in London, Adelaide and San Francisco. The IMW also holds seminars and course days in Australia, Austria, France, Germany, the US and the UK, where existing MWs offer aspirants guidance and advice on how to prepare for the exam. Every student on the programme is assigned an MW mentor who reviews their assignments and progress.

Not everyone who takes the exam goes on to become an MW. The IMW does not publish its pass rates, but rumour is that they are notoriously low; often on the lower side of single digits. Many candidates take several years and multiple tries to pass all three stages of the programme. Earning the title is considered one of the most challenging achievements in the wine industry.

The MW is a self-directed study programme where it is up to the student to ensure that they are fully prepared in all aspects of the exam. Studying for the MW demands sacrifice, commitment and perseverance. It is not for the faint-hearted. The exams test your knowledge and understanding of wine with a fine-toothed comb. They require extensive studying, and the tasting and evaluation of wines from different regions, producers and vintages. Those who embark on this journey need to demonstrate a high level of expertise and knowledge through countless hours of learning, tasting and practising.

Being on the MW programme can be an isolating process, especially for those who do not come from wine families. Candidates often end up feeling alone as their closest friends and family may fail to understand the significance of the pursuit. So, apart from testing your knowledge, the MW programme also tests your grit, patience and mental strength to stay the course.

However, once you achieve the title, there are great benefits too. Becoming an MW means entry into an elite wine community. It brings enriching personal and professional opportunities that are both unique and exclusive. MWs are renowned tasters who are regularly asked to judge wine competitions all over the world, to lecture on wine courses and to assess some of the world's finest wine cellars. They command unequivocal respect from the global wine industry and uncontested authority in their domain.

My decision to become an MW was perhaps ahead of its time. India was neither known for its winemaking nor for its levels of wine consumption. India was yet to truly assume its place in the wine world. It never featured in the WSET syllabus, nor were we expected to know any data points about India for the purpose of the exam. Since our country was not prominent on the global wine map, having an MW from India was unusual. In fact, in 2010—when I enrolled for the programme—Italy, one of the top three wine producers in the world, and China, which had a relatively bigger wine market and industry than ours, still didn't have an MW. So, I suppose an Indian MW may not have been on anybody's radar. I had quietly entered the programme without garnering any attention or raising any expectations.

However, the IMW is committed to fostering a culture of diversity, inclusion and ongoing transformations. They are keen to ensure that the composition of their membership truly reflects the variety within the industry in which they operate. Regardless of your ethnicity, gender or complexion, the IMW ensures everyone on the programme feels welcome and is adequately supported throughout. India is an intriguing market with an illustrious past, rich culture and a current trajectory of enviable economic growth. Today, being an Indian in a room will earn you recognition for being the contributor of a fresh new perspective. Perhaps, as an Indian on the programme, I represented not just heterogeneity but also a disruption of sorts.

I must emphasise here that as an Indian student, I was never made to feel less in any way. The programme is equally rigorous for all students and there is no bias of any sort, one way or the other. Regardless of who you are and where you come from, the MW exam remains among the toughest exam in the world and you better brace yourself for it.

8

Two Hundred Wines and a Wedding

Having just finished my diploma, my theoretical knowledge was fresh and sound, but I felt that I needed more on-ground real-world experience, especially given how new I was to wine. On-field experience was a strong suit for many of the other candidates, who had done extensive wine-related work or travel.

While I couldn't start working at a vineyard at this point in my personal and professional life, I figured I could cover considerable ground with travel. I had known that I would have to make sacrifices on this journey, but I hadn't realised how soon I would have to start making difficult choices.

In 2011, I signed up for an extensive tour of all the wine regions of Australia. The tour was organised by MW Tim Wildman's travel company, James Busby Travel. Named after 'the father of the Australian wine industry', it promised to take 'wine trade professionals on the ultimate Australian road trip'.[9] The two-

---

[9] Fergal Gleeson, 'Australian Wine Trailblazers', *Great Wine Blog*, https://greatwineblog.com/portfolio/australian-wine-trailblazers/; https://jamesbusbytravel.com/.

week-long tour had hit the road just the previous year and was a huge hit, especially among students and wine enthusiasts.

I signed up for the trip, thinking it would earn me a lot of hands-on experience of and better knowledge of winemaking and the rich and abundant wine culture of Australia, one of the most prominent wine regions in the world. I booked my seat on the tour six months in advance.

Three months before the tour, I got a call from my childhood friend, Mallika. Along with our friend Sharmin, we were known as 'the three musketeers'. Sharmin and I were each others soulmates while Mallika was our dearest bosom buddy. Mallika used to drive around in a flashy car when we were in college, making her the designated driver for all trips and parties. The three of us used to take long drives together, blasting music and singing along until our throats hurt. Everyone has songs that they associate with different eras of their lives. I still have a playlist of all the songs that we would listen to in Mallika's car, and it takes me back to my days of being a carefree youngster with not a worry in the world.

It's not as though I was in touch with Mallika on a regular basis, but the beauty of childhood friendships is that you can pick up from where you left off, even if you haven't spoken in months. Mallika knew that I was pursuing an MW and I knew that she had a steady boyfriend. I just didn't realise how fast things were moving in her relationship.

'Hozefa and I are getting married in three months, Sonal!' she announced.

'Wow! That's out of the blue, Mallika. Congratulations!' I squealed.

'I'll need my besties by my side, so clear your schedule.'

'That goes without saying! So, when is the big day?'

'It's in October. It's going to be a week-long celebration.'

'Okay, what are the dates?' I asked.

As soon as she told me the dates, I felt all the excitement drain from my body—they coincided with the dates of my Australian wine tour. There was no point in getting her hopes high and ditching her at the last hour. So, I decided to come clean at that very moment.

'Mallika, darling I don't know how else to say this, but I am not here on those days,' I said apologetically.

'What do you mean?'

'I have signed up for this educational trip to Australia. It's on the same dates.'

'I don't give a shit about your trip! Just cancel it!' Mallika exclaimed. Imagine having to convince your best friend to come to your wedding instead of going on a tour of Australia.

'I can't do that, Mallika. It's an important study trip,' I reasoned.

'How can it be more important than my wedding, Sonal? What are you even going to do there?'

'You don't understand, Mallika. I am going to learn about Australian wines.'

'Well, that can be done anytime. Why do you have to do it when I am getting married?'

'It's very difficult to get a seat on that tour, and it will really help with my MW studies. The tour is being conducted by an MW himself and they will take us to some of the greatest wineries in the region.'

I heard Mallika sigh and pause on the other end of the line. She was frustrated with me and didn't understand my need to go on this trip.

'I'm so sorry, Mallika, sounds like I'm going to miss your wedding.'

She was pissed, and hung up without another word. Now, it's not as if I couldn't have cancelled my trip and claimed a refund or tried getting a seat on the tour next year. But I was so committed to the cause that it didn't even occur to me for a second that I should cancel my booking and go to my friend's wedding instead. This incident is the perfect example of the kind of passion and single-minded focus that each MW must have. Nothing else in the world matters.

Obviously, my friend has held this grudge against me for years. In fact, we had a conversation about it just recently.

'Sonal, it's not the fact that you didn't come. It's the fact that you showed no remorse. You never said that you'd at least think about your decision or try to postpone the trip. You refused to attend the wedding outright and instantly, it was as if I never stood a chance against your Australia trip.'

'I am so sorry, Mallika,' I apologised again, 'I was in a different phase of my life then. I was a mom and wife; I had given up a good career to do something no one understood. I prioritised my professional dreams over our friendship; there's no other way to put it, but hey, we didn't give up on our friendship.'

'Lovely words, Sonal. But you missed my wedding and I'll hold this over your head for the rest of your life,' Mallika said. Both of us burst out laughing. Careers, life-altering decisions, husbands and children have put us on different paths, but we have indeed found our way back. I guess, that's what real friendship means—you always pick up from where you leave off and move ahead, with or without holding a grudge, or a proverbial dagger in this case.

While the Australia trip nearly cost me a dear friendship, I still hold it in high regard. It was one of the most enriching educational trips I have ever taken.

This was a fourteen-day road trip across the southern belt of mighty Australia, traversing the country from east to west. All the travellers gathered at a hotel in Sydney where Tim introduced each one of us. I looked at a bunch of strangers staring awkwardly at each other and realised I didn't know anybody in the room.

Dear God, why have I signed up to spend fourteen days with this group of people? None of them seems to be approachable enough to become friends with, I thought. I was bored already. *Why am I here? Why am I not at home, chilling with Rianna and Andrew? Why did I give up on my best friend's wedding to be here? How am I going to survive the next fourteen days? What is wrong with me?*

But it is amazing what time and proximity can do. We spent most of the trip cooped up in a bus, travelling across the glorious Australian landscape. Mind you, we didn't have high-tech smartphones or even affordable wifi access to pass the time, so the only thing left to do was talk to the person sitting next to you or crack a joke that would make everyone laugh and eventually break the ice.

Tim had a brilliant idea—he announced on the first day that the funniest joke told during the tour would get a prize. With nothing else to do, we all took up the challenge. We all let our guards down and talked a lot of rubbish.

On a more serious note, we visited two to three wineries each day, making it a total of over thirty wineries, and tasted over 200 wines on this entire trip. We would spend nights in hotels to give our backs a break after sitting in the bus all day. Since we had to travel light, we would repeat our outfits without washing them. Our scruffy state made us cherish the evenings we spent relaxing at hotels, where we could open a few bottles of wine, chat and get a bit rowdy. That's how we got to discover each other's crazy talents and real aspirations.

We visited some of Australia's most iconic wineries. Starting with the east coast, we visited Tyrells, an excellent winery that makes Australia's most awarded white wines from the Semillon grape. Here, we learnt how a relatively neutral and non-aromatic grape variety can transform into something ethereal and complex with age, giving smoky and toasty notes even without any oak ageing. Semillon from here is a global benchmark, and this wine style often appears in the MW exams, where students mistake it for an oak-aged Chardonnay.

A memorable visit on the tour was to Penfolds Magill Estate, the most esteemed winery in South Australia, founded in 1844. Today, Penfolds, a prestigious Australian wine brand that also enjoys fame in India, has wineries in California, France and China. But, the magic and legacy of the Magill Estate in Adelaide remains unparalleled.

To understand what makes Magill Estate so special, we have to go back to the end of the nineteenth century, when winemaking was at a nascent stage on the continent. A deadly infestation of a microscopic louse called phylloxera was wreaking havoc in vineyards across the world. The louse, known to live and eat the roots of grape vines, spread rapidly from one continent to the other. In a desperate attempt to stop the spread, vineyard owners ripped out vines from the ground or burnt them, but to no avail. By the beginning of the new century, the infestation had claimed seventy per cent of vines in Europe, posing a threat to the existence of the wine industry. However, there was an exception.

The phylloxera infestation hadn't spread as aggressively across the vast Australian continent with vineyards located at greater distances, as it did in wine-centric Europe or California. As a result, South Australia managed to preserve historic rootstock that had largely vanished from the rest of the world. Today, Australia is home to some of the world's oldest vines of popular grape varieties like Shiraz, Cabernet Sauvignon, Mourvèdre and Grenache, some of which are over 125 years old! These old vines yield lower quantities of fruit compared to their younger counterparts, but the grapes are packed with divine flavours that give the wines a memorable flavour profile.

You can understand how excited we must have been to see these old vines that had preserved a part of winemaking history in their roots. But the highlight of that visit was meeting Penfolds Chief Winemaker Peter Gago, who holds a legendary status for his dedication to preserving old vines and making award-winning wines. A chemistry and mathematics teacher who eventually succumbed to his long-held interest in wine, Peter has been recognised for his work in the Australian wine industry, becoming South Australia's Great Wine Capitals Global Ambassador and receiving his appointment as a Companion of the Order of Australia. He conducted a tasting session for us. It was a huge honour to taste some old vintages of Penfolds wines including the iconic Penfolds Grange, learn about Australian wines from him and just bask in his presence.

We also visited Henschke—one of the oldest family-owned wineries in Eden Valley and tasted Hill of Grace, a renowned single-vineyard Shiraz wine known for its exceptional quality and heritage. At the Yalumba Wine Estates in the Barossa Valley, it was fascinating to see how oak barrels are made at their family-owned cooperages.

Another memorable visit was to Paxton Wines in the McLaren Vale region. Paxton is an organic and biodynamic winery. The practice of biodynamics relies on a strong connection between the position of the stars, planets and the moon and the practice of sustainable agriculture. One of the interesting practices we observed at the winery involved filling cow horns with cow dung and burying them in the soil to fertilise it. The winery believes this practice yields a purer expression of the grape variety than that grown using modern agricultural techniques. While the winemaker was seriously explaining the process to us, I joked, 'If this practice is anything to go by, then India has been practising biodynamic agriculture since the dawn of time. The wine industry would thrive in India because there is no shortage of cow dung there!'

While I said it in a lighter tone, this wasn't far from the truth. The concept of biodynamics was introduced in 1920s by the Austrian philosopher Rudolph Steiner, but Indian farmers have practised it for centuries, following lunisolar calendars to guide them through different stages of agriculture, from sowing to harvesting. It was fascinating to see how agricultural practices have spread across the boundaries of language and time, making themselves visible in different forms in different regions, but with ancient wisdom and the power of observation at their heart. I couldn't help but wonder how practices like organic farming and biodynamics have been a part of Indian heritage for years, and are just now being rediscovered by scientists and agriculturists in the West.

The trip trailed across the southern regions of Australia and concluded at the Cape Mentelle winery located near the Margaret river of Western Australia. This is one of the region's 'founding five' wineries that today boasts of having mature vineyards, and are known for producing benchmark styles of wines from Cabernet Sauvignon and Chardonnay grape varieties that regularly scoop up awards at international wine competitions.

The Australian tour wove many such memorable explorations together to enrich my understanding of wine. I had first-hand exposure to the diversity and quality of Australian winemaking. It was the first time I got to observe winemaking outside of textbooks, which gave me real-life examples to use later in my theory papers. But, like the 'old vines', the trip bore a sweeter and rarer fruit—that of unexpected friendships. The group became like a family away from family, and while I don't remember who won the prize for cracking the best joke, just thinking about all my mates brings a smile to my lips.

On the last day of the tour, we were all crying and hugging each other, promising to stay in touch forever. But as life would have it, we all drifted apart once we got back to our respective routines and countries. However, there's one fellow traveller who remains a close friend even today: Richard Hemming MW. A fellow MW aspirant, Richard became an inseparable friend on the trip and we have stayed in touch, often updating each other about our progress, setbacks and struggles.

'We'll start a venture together. Holland and Hemming for world domination!' I would tell him.

'Oh yes! But why do you always put your Holland before my Hemming?' he would ask.

'Because that's how it's meant to be.'

Nonetheless, Hemming beat Holland to the finish line when he became an MW in 2015.

At the end of the first year of the MW programme, students have to sit for the Stage 1 Assessment (S1A) exam, which is like a preliminary exam to determine whether or not they are ready to take the main theory and blind-tasting papers. It consists of one twelve-wine blind tasting paper and two theory essays.

If you fail this test, the IMW requests you to withdraw from the programme and re-apply a few years later. This helps the institute sieve out candidates with little to no chance of passing the main exams. Such candidates can either move on to something else or focus on gaining more industry experience and knowledge.

Despite my initial difficulties and the embarrassing tasting sessions during the inaugural week, I passed the first-year exam. It boosted my confidence—maybe this wasn't as difficult as I had thought it to be. But it turned out that first-year exams were also the gateway to another level of difficulty where the heat is turned up by several degrees.

'And then there's Sonal ...'

Richard Hemming MW, a friend of Sonal's

It's much better to be memorable than normal. Most of the world's wines are normal: simple, safe, familiar. They do their job, but in an unremarkable way. By the same token, most of the world's people are normal too.

And then there's Sonal.

We met on the first day of a two-week tour of Australian vineyards, back in 2011: a group of twelve complete strangers from the wine trade, thrown together on a minibus with a bottomless supply of wine. If anyone started that trip as a normal person, they didn't stay that way for long.

Sonal was memorable from the outset: charismatic, strong-willed and wickedly funny, with a laugh that could silence the kookaburras.

She was busy establishing herself as the preeminent voice on wine within India, despite having started that journey relatively recently. Not only that, she had ambitions to reach the very top of the industry by embarking on the notoriously difficult Master of Wine qualification. At the time, wine culture in India was in its infancy, so this would be no mean feat: Sonal loved to tell us that per capita wine consumption in her home country was less than one teaspoon per person per year—and that she was going to double it.

We became firm friends during that Australia tour. Her charisma, firmly held opinions and uniquely Indian perspective always led to the most lively and interesting conversations. I learnt and I laughed in equal measure. As a fellow wine professional, I was in awe of her ability to ask the sort of challenging questions that most people wouldn't dare to ask. She always afforded wine the respect it deserves, but with a healthy dash of irreverence.

Since then, we have shared many more moments over some wonderful wines at the clubs, bars and restaurants of London; while touring the vineyards of Nashik; at each other's homes, and at wine trade gatherings around the world. As a host, Sonal's generosity knows no bounds; as a guest she is always invigorating company.

Attaining the MW qualification in 2016 was a definitive moment not only for Sonal's career but for the story of wine in India. Wherever wine is poured there, Sonal's influence is surely never far away. Her career covers a range of wine activities as diverse as wine itself, from retail to education to consultancy, underlining both her entrepreneurial spirit and her adaptability. The success of her business is delightful to see, and should be a surprise to nobody that knows her.

It is an honour to call Sonal both a friend and a colleague in the wine trade. The world of wine relies on such personalities to keep it alive: people that are dynamic, driven and, above all, memorable.

9

When the Going Gets Tough

I was now at Stage 2 of the programme, which consisted of both theory and tasting exams. At that time, the MW exams consisted of four theory papers:

- Viticulture: tests you on the science of growing grapes and everything that happens in the vineyard up until the harvest and the process of the grapes being taken into the winery;

- Vinification and pre-bottling procedures: examines your knowledge of vinification of still, sparkling and fortified wine through all steps up to the stage of being ready for bottling;

- Handling of wine: tests you on bottling processes, quality assurance, quality control, packaging options, transport and regulatory requirements, etc. for wine;

- Business of wine: evaluates your understanding of current financial, commercial and marketing aspects of the international wine industry.

Each of these subjects is tested in a two-and-a-quarter-hour exam, where you are expected to provide critical analysis of the subjects, including relevant examples to demonstrate in-depth understanding rather than simply bookish knowledge.

The questions asked in the exam are often open-ended, for example: 'Discuss the role of water in the production of high-quality wines'. Here, you will have to write a 1,000–1,200-word essay, considering the pros, the cons and the prospects, with all your inferences based on global examples. This means that you would need to know the climate, geography, topography and viticulture practices of different wine regions of the world and how the presence of water bodies like rivers, oceans or lakes and rainfall or irrigation affect the production of wine. You would also have to know all the high-quality wine regions of the world and the influence of water on wine production there, giving examples of what specific wine producers do in their vineyards.

Along with having subject knowledge, the IMW also expects students to write the answers in a specific essay format which requires exceptional journalistic writing. This can pose a high level of difficulty for anyone whose first language isn't English. Despite being a convent-educated girl from Mumbai, I felt my schooling had not prepared me to write such answers. How was I supposed to write top-notch prose to pass the theory exams?

And the tasting exams are an entirely different beast. Spread over three days, students are given twelve white wines to analyse on day one, followed by twelve reds on day two and a mixed bag on day three, which could have still wines, sparkling wines, rosés, white and red wines, fortified wines and sweet wines. These exams don't involve merely blind-tasting and identification of wines. Usually, students get a key during the exam that could either decode the whole tasting or leave them more confused than ever.

For context, here's a question from Paper 2 of the blind-tasting exam from 2022:[10]

---

[10] 'Institute of Masters of Wine Master of Wine Exam 2022', *Bottle Bank*, https://www.bottlebank.com/a-complete-guide-to-the-2022-master-of-wine-exam-mw-from-the-institute-of-masters-of-wine/.

Wines 1-3 are from different countries and are each made from a different, single grape variety. Wine 4 is a blend of all three of these varieties.

For each wine 1-3:

a) Identify the grape variety and the origin as closely as possible. (3*15 marks)

b) Comment on the style, considering possible reasons for not blending the variety used for this wine. (3*10 marks)

For wine 4:

c) Comment on the purpose of blending these varieties with reference to balance and quality. (15 marks)

d) Identify the origin as closely as possible. (10 marks)

Now, here's how as an MW student, I am expected to answer this question.

I must first consider the clue given in the question itself. All four wines on this flight (a selection of wines with something in common; such as the producer, grape variety, region; these are presented in a row) are connected by three grape varieties, and wine 4 is, in fact, a blend of these three grape varieties. This means we are looking for grape varieties that are commonly used for making wines on their own as well as used in blends. This automatically narrows down my choices, as not every grape variety is typically used in a blend, and there are some blends that are classics in the wine world. For example, a blend of Cabernet Sauvignon, Merlot and Cabernet Franc is used in Bordeaux; a blend of Grenache, Syrah and Mouvedre is made in the Rhone Valley; a Sangiovese is blended with Merlot and Cabernet Sauvignon in the Tuscany region. All these could be plausible answers, since these grape varieties, while used successfully in blends, can also be used for making single varietal wines.

With these mental notes of possible grape varieties, I must start tasting, analysing the colour, aromas, mouthfeel and flavours of the wine. For example, high searing acidity and grippy tannins will automatically rule out Grenache, which has medium-level round acidity and comparatively softer tannins. This way, through tasting and applying my knowledge of the grape varieties, I will be able to narrow down my choices. Some typical aromas and flavours like blackcurrants and bell peppers in a Cabernet Sauvignon, plums in Merlot, tea-like savoury notes of Sangiovese and black pepper and spice in Syrah will also lead me towards certain grape varieties.

Once you have the grape varieties, the origins of the wine can lead you to deduce wine 4, because Grenache, Syrah and Mouvedre can either be a Chateuneuf-du-Pape if it's a high-quality wine, or a Southern Rhone blend if it is an average quality wine. Quality must also be assessed through tasting the wine for its fineness of balance, length, complexity and intensity of flavours. Through competent tasting, the maze will start to reveal itself, and once the picture becomes clearer, you will be able to reach some decision on what you think the three individual wines are and how they come together in a blend for wine 4.

However, simply offering a conclusive answer in the written notes is not enough. I must use the evidence in the glass to demonstrate that I have considered all possible choices backed by theoretical information, funnelling down to one right answer, by eliminating each of the alternatives with further evidence. The conclusion must neatly tie up all the evidence to present the most probable answer to the question. Funnelling down and arguing your case requires accurate tasting skills, theoretical knowledge as well as the use of logical reasoning.

I will have to identify wine 4 correctly. If I got that one wrong, it could have a domino effect on wines 1 to 3 and the rest of my answer will be entirely incorrect. Using illogical choices like Pinot Noir, which is almost never used in blends, would be considered fatal, as this would instantly expose a lack of theoretical knowledge.

This is just an example of how students have to continuously draw evidence for identifying the wine in the glass through tasting, analysis and deductive answers. Each paper has twelve wines, so you may have to analyse close to three to four wine flights per paper. There are three such days of tastings, with twelve wines per day that you have to try and get through calmly. You barely get two minutes per wine for tasting; any longer and you just wouldn't be left with enough time to write the answers.

The MW tasting exam can really play tricks on your mind. Every wine can look and taste the same, and students are often tempted to shoehorn an answer due to confirmation bias. Another big challenge is not being able to taste the wine accurately or not having enough knowledge to support your inferences. There is no remedy for poor tasting skills or limited wine knowledge.

You must pass either all the theory papers or all the tasting papers in your first three attempts, and only then can you continue with the programme. If you neither clear all the theory papers nor tasting papers and exhaust all your tries, you are taken off it. The IMW supports you by assessing your submissions on which it offers feedback to help you keep track of your progress.

This was a crucial phase that required me to study really hard. Putting everything aside, I read every book anyone recommended to me. I went over all my diploma notes and purchased at least two dozen books recommended by the IMW. Since most of these books were unavailable in India, I would order them from Amazon UK or purchase them from London bookstores. Some of the most memorable books that I read to prepare for my exams are *The World Atlas of Wine*, *The Oxford Companion to Wine* and other books by Jancis Robinson, *Wine Science: The Application of Science in Winemaking* by Jamie Goode, *Understanding Wine Technology* by David Bird and *Wine Myths and Reality* by Benjamin Lewin. I also read country-specific books that covered wine regions like Napa Valley, Bordeaux and Burgundy.

I would be hunched over my books for hours, simultaneously looking after my toddler daughter, who was yet to start preschool. There were sleepless nights with fevers, coughs and stomach upsets that required me to be by her side all the time. Besides, I had vowed that no matter how tough life became, Rianna would always be my top priority. A child of her age deserved all the attention she could get from her mother, and if that meant waking up at ungodly hours to study, or quickly scanning through a chapter while she took her nap, then so be it.

The only time I would step out of my house was to attend tasting events and dinners as they helped with the learning and in keeping up appearances in the wine industry in order to stay relevant. As a result, any social life I had outside of the wine world became non-existent. I would dodge calls from friends and decline invitations to gatherings and brunches from extended family. Although there was no way out of certain social engagements, every second I spent away from my studies weighed on me. I could hear the clock ticking in my head, taunting me that I was wasting my time and that I would pay dearly for this frivolity.

There were serious limitations on how many wines I could taste while living in India. Most of the premium examples of classic wines were either not being imported here or were out of stock in an importer's portfolio. So, I had to make sure I remembered the wines I tasted when I travelled. Some wines

I must have sampled only once or twice, then memorised the tasting notes and written them down in detail for revision later. Basically, I learnt some wines by rote.

Students who have prepared for any kind of competitive exam will understand what I mean. That sense of dread you feel every time someone else tells you how amazing their prep is going. The nights spent tossing and turning, resenting your body's need for rest, only to feel tired and irritated throughout the day. Reading till your eyes are sore and letters have started merging into one another.

In my first attempt, I managed to clear three of the four theory papers but I royally flunked the tasting exams. While I was dejected at the failure, I found solace in the fact that I seemed to be on the right track. Besides, the IMW offers students who have failed just one paper a chance to retake that subject in the subsequent year (along with the tasting papers), instead of having to resit for exams in all the subjects. But this is a one-time chance, so if you blow this opportunity, you have to take all the theory papers again (along with the tasting exams, if you have failed to clear them as well).

In 2013, I was planning to put in a lot of hard work to ensure that I passed the single theory paper I had failed, and retake the tasting exams. Since I had three fewer papers to worry about, I thought it was manageable.

Around this time, I got a call from Taljinder Singh, vice president of food and beverages at ITC Hotels. He told me he wanted to hire someone to head their wine and beverage programme.

'We have been considering a few people from overseas, but your name came recommended through Kapil Sekhri, founder of Fratelli Vineyards. I believe that you have some top qualifications in wine and we would like to pursue a discussion with you to see if you'd like to head our wine and beverage programme,' he said.

I was flattered to get this opportunity. I asked, 'Is this a full-time role or are you calling me to join as a consultant?'

'No ma'am, it's a full-time position. Would you be open to relocating to New Delhi as we are headquartered here?'

'I'm afraid I can't do that. I have a family here in Mumbai and my daughter is just four years old. Relocating won't be possible for me,' I said. 'But if you're willing, I can be based out of one of your Mumbai hotels and travel to Delhi as and when needed,' I added.

I went through a couple of rounds of interviews, including one with Dipak Haksar, the CEO of ITC Hotels at the time, and was made a lucrative offer. They also generously accepted my terms and conditions and allowed me to work out of Mumbai so that I could live with my family. I was free to operate between ITC Grand Central in Lower Parel and ITC Maratha in Andheri East.

I was very excited to start working at ITC Hotels. I felt very fortunate to head the wine and beverage programme for a chain of over a hundred hotels in India; an opportunity that typically only falls into the lap of MWs, and here I was getting to do this even before becoming one. My main responsibilities here were to enhance the knowledge, skills and confidence of the F&B staff through training sessions, to enhance the wine offerings at their specialty restaurants and to curate events that positioned ITC among the finest hotels in the country.

The three years I spent at ITC taught me much and gave me tremendous confidence and experience as a wine professional. I built a robust training programme there and created the single largest pool of WSET-qualified wine professionals in the country with over a hundred ITC employees. It felt like a victory of my undying belief in the importance of wine education. 'Finally, an

organisation that believes in the value of training its employees,'
I thought feeling a sense of vindication.

Working with ITC Hotels also made me commercially
relevant. Suddenly, I started getting calls from wine importers
and producers from around the country who wanted to meet
me and take me out to lunches. They would offer me wines
for tasting, hoping that I would approve some of them and get
them listed in the wine lists of the hotels. By taking up this job, I
had become a gatekeeper and purchase influencer for the hotel
chain—quite a powerful position to hold. I felt like my career
was suddenly taking off.

Things got busier, as I started curating events at ITC
restaurants. I would spend the day working at the office and
in the evening host events for consumers interested in tasting
and learning more about wine. We once had the pleasure of
welcoming at the hotel Mr Pablo Alvarez, CEO of Vega Sicilia,
one of the most prestigious wineries of Spain. We hosted a series
of media tastings and wine dinners for consumers in Mumbai
and Delhi, who paid for a seat at the table to drink wines that are
highly sought after by connoisseurs and collectors worldwide.

While all this was happening, I found myself juggling
motherhood, work and studies. It was a tough balancing act.
Perhaps I prioritised my studies a bit less than the job, and that's
where I took the hit.

Two weeks before the exam, reality dawned—I hadn't studied
enough. I reached London a week before the exams and decided
cramming my notes and tasting as many wines as I could was my
best bet. This meant virtually no sleep. As a result, my immune
system weakened and I developed a cough and cold. As you can
imagine, a blocked nose is the worst thing that could happen to
a student just before the tasting exams, as your ability to analyse
a wine goes for a toss. I was doomed to fail.

I wasn't surprised that I failed that one theory exam and all the tasting papers. Reflecting on it, I realised I had bitten off more than I could chew by taking up a full-time job at the ITC while pursuing the title.

I was now back at the bottom of the ladder. From having a comfortable shot at the title, I had landed in a do-or-die situation. I would have to take all four theory exams again. Moreover, I would also have to pass either the entire theory block or the tasting block in my next attempt. Or else, I was out. I was on my last chance to make the MW happen.

I was down and out, and my confidence had hit rock bottom. So, I started seeking an escape. The IMW allows students to take a year off anytime during the programme, in case they need a cool-off period. I seriously considered doing that.

I told Andrew, 'All I have left is this one chance. I can't afford to blow it. Shall I take a year off?'

'What difference will a break year make?' he asked.

'Maybe I'm just saturated with my studies. Taking time off will help me regain focus.'

Like any good coach, Andrew refused to let me slip. 'I don't think that's a good idea. You will lose all the momentum you've gained. You've got this, Sonal. You're just one final push away from crossing that finish line; don't lose faith in yourself now. I am here to support you, and we will do what it takes.'

I wasn't happy but I decided to move forward anyway, focusing equally on my job and my studies.

Days before my third attempt at the Stage 2 exams, I was feeling terribly homesick because it was Rianna's fifth birthday and I was about to miss it. When kids are young, these milestone birthdays are a source of immense joy and pride for every parent. I had flown to London a few days before my exams to get away from all the distractions. But as Rianna's birthday approached,

I felt overcome with guilt and pangs of maternal love. I called Andrew to give him grief.

'Andrew, I'm about to book a ticket back to Mumbai. It'll be a quick two-day trip. I don't think it will impact my studies and I'll get to be with Rianna on her birthday,' I announced.

'That's quite sudden. What happened?' he asked, obviously alarmed at this impulsive decision.

'I just miss home! I want to be with Rianna and you, even if it's just for a couple of hours.'

'I get it, but this trip will be a huge distraction, Sonal. Don't feel bad about missing her birthday.'

'No, this is terrible, Andrew. This is too much. I can't be away from her on her fifth birthday; it's such a special day for her.'

'Let's not book tickets right away, Sonal. Why don't you sleep on this? Maybe you'll feel differently tomorrow. We'll do a video call and you won't feel like you're missing out.'

I didn't book my tickets. Maybe Andrew was right and I would feel differently if I tried to sleep off my homesickness.

Next morning, I was still in bed when the doorbell rang. Thinking that it must be housekeeping, I got out of bed and opened the door to my hotel room. I thought I was dreaming when I saw little Rianna standing in the doorway, carrying three balloons in her hand.

I couldn't believe my eyes! There she was, my little girl looking at me with a huge smile on her face. Andrew poked his head into the doorway and said softly, 'Surprise! We knew how much you were missing us and how important it is for you to study, so we took the overnight flight to come and see you.'

Had I booked my tickets the night before, I would have spent the next two days travelling from London to Mumbai and back, and then two more days reeling from the hectic travel and time difference. But Andrew knew how important it was for me to stay focused, so he dropped everything and flew to London with Rianna to cheer me up. This is just one of the many gestures with which Andrew ensured that I wasn't distracted or tired for my exams. I felt so energised after their visit. My confidence was back.

I took the theory exams in my final attempt and I passed all my papers. I jokingly tell everyone that I have cleared MW twice because I had to once more clear the papers I had passed previously. So, in effect, I had passed seven papers instead of four. Unfortunately, I had failed the tasting for the third time in a row. But I was relieved that I would get more chances to tame that beast. What happened to me isn't uncommon. A lot of students have to choose their poison and focus on either the theory or the tasting exams, instead of fighting the battle on both fronts and losing altogether.

Every MW student must have a sense of absolute determination. If you are already looking at other options or thinking of a life where you haven't won a title, then you'll never be able to commit yourself fully to the cause. You must tell yourselves that there is no plan B; failure is not an option.

Despite the eventful four years, I was only halfway through the programme. But I didn't intend to take it slow anymore. I was going to approach the tasting exams in top gear.

10

Tastebuds on Fire

All I did the following year was to taste as many wines as I could. The kind of high-quality and versatile wines that appeared in the exams were not available in India, so, I had to travel extensively to refine my wine palate. This meant living out of a suitcase and travelling through every wine-producing region of the world, visiting endless vineyards, meeting hundreds of wine producers and attending every tasting event I could find a seat at.

The IMW organised practice sessions at their London-based institute. Now that the theory was out of the way, I could make the most of these sessions. These day-long sessions involved tasting a flight of twelve wines. The students would then write their observations and get direct feedback on their answers. The IMW would invite MWs to conduct these tasting sessions.

As soon as these sessions were announced, I would sign up for them and drop everything to fly to London. While these were all optional, they were a boon for me, and I felt I couldn't afford to miss out on any of them if I wanted to clear the tasting exams.

Since I was spending a considerable amount of money to travel to London for the MW tastings, it made sense to extend my stay by a few days and make the most of the trip. I would visit bars and restaurants in the city to taste more wines. I remember walking into a bar in London once and telling the bartender that I would buy twenty-five bottles of wine from him. I then persuaded him to give me a substantial discount, as I just needed a few sips from each bottle, after which he could sell the remaining wine by the glass to his patrons. In that last year, I pulled out all the stops for every opportunity I could find to taste wine.

Large trade shows like Vinexpo, the London Wine Fair and ProWine were also a great way to taste more wines. I would study the schedule of all the trade shows happening throughout the year and then figure out which ones I could afford to attend. For instance, Vinexpo organised trade fairs in cities like Paris, New York, Amsterdam, Hong Kong and Singapore and I tried to attend as many as I could.

I would register as an MW student and walk around these huge trade shows alongside thousands of visitors. Some exhibitors would kindly pour a glass of wine for me, and a few would be kinder and even discuss the style of wine with me, taking me through the winemaking process used. This was extremely important, as the MW exam wasn't just about knowing the taste of a particular wine but knowing every possible detail about how it was made.

Trade shows are a great place to forge new business relationships and showcase your labels to an eager audience of industry professionals and consumers. You can get direct feedback alongside a snapshot of the current market landscape. From the latest innovations in the field to marketing trends and thought-provoking conversations on sustainability, trade shows have a lot to offer, and I absorbed everything in addition to the wines I tasted.

Many of my fellow MW aspirants also played a significant role in helping me with wine tasting while being valuable companions in an otherwise lonely journey. One such friend is Elisa Kwon de Álvarez, who is married to Pablo Álvarez—the CEO of Vega Sicilia, whom I had hosted at the ITC. Elisa became a good friend while we were on the programme together. One day, while catching up, the conversation naturally turned to our MW exam preparation, and I told her about my struggles.

'Why don't you come to live with me for a couple of weeks, Sonal? We can study together and go visit wineries all over Spain,' she said.

As I was eager to learn about Spanish wines, I couldn't refuse her generous offer. 'Are you sure, Elisa? Because I have no reason to decline this amazing offer,' I joked.

'Of course! Let's do this.'

So without wasting a moment, I booked my tickets and appeared on Elisa's doorstep. As I had expected, I received a warm welcome. It was thrilling to live under the same roof as Pablo Alvarez, so imagine my joy when the icon took over the kitchen one night to whip up a delicious pasta with prawns in arrabbiata sauce using his grandmother's recipe!

'No one can make an arrabbiata sauce like my grandmother,' he claimed. Indeed, I had never tasted anything like it. I can still taste that velvety and aromatic sauce, bursting with flavours of juicy Italian tomatoes and fresh herbs; it was truly exquisite and remains the best tomato sauce I've ever had with pasta.

Elisa and I travelled to numerous wineries across the country, and all the doors just magically opened for us thanks to the reverence her husband enjoyed in the industry. Winemakers would give us a tour of their facilities, discussing their process and sharing their winemaking knowledge, and they would happily pour their finest wines for us.

I spent a lot of time with Elisa's lovely three-year-old daughter named Valentina. Playing with her and feeling her tiny arms wrapped around my neck as she hugged me lovingly made me miss Rianna, who was only slightly older. I would console myself that while I was away from my child, I had Valentina to keep me company, so I should make the most of this opportunity.

The kindness and hospitality of the Alvarez family is a memory that I cherish even today. But come to think of it, I wouldn't have made all these wonderful connections or enjoyed Spanish hospitality had it not been for the MW journey.

Another friend I made during my MW years is Catherine Wallace, who lived in Central London back in the day. Catherine was an excellent taster, and I wanted to learn her process. So, one day I said to her, 'Catherine, I wish I could spend more time with you because I could really learn something from tasting wines with you.'

'Sure, the next time you are in London, why don't you stay with me?'

She welcomed me wholeheartedly, letting me stay in the spare room of her two-bedroom London flat on multiple occasions. I would repay her kindness by cooking for her and her partner, gifting them Indian masalas and taking them out for meals. During my stay, each of us would pick a wine for the other and do a tasting session to test our skills. Once we were done, we would curl up in her living room, pour big glasses of the wines we had tasted earlier and talk non-stop about our lives, motivations and goals.

I learnt a lot from Catherine, but she didn't make it as an MW, and neither did Elisa. It pained me to see my friends drop out of the programme. In those six years at IMW, I watched many acquaintances either drop out or run out of attempts. It was scary and heartbreaking—I could envision the race track around me emptying, increasing my sense of isolation. These were people who understood what I was going through, and each one of us had a valid and equally compelling desire to become an MW.

But there's nothing you can do to change another student's fate. The MW isn't ranked on a percentile scale—every candidate is racing against themselves, their circumstances and choices, testing the limits of their grit and patience. Sometimes, despite having the right background, financial security, determination and motivation, people don't make it. Many candidates who drop out of the MW programme go on to establish themselves as successful wine professionals nonetheless. The title may be a path to success, but it is certainly not the only one.

However, some candidates beat all odds and predictions to emerge victorious. One such underdog in the MW race was Almudena Alberca, whom we used to fondly call Almu. Almu began her career as an assistant winemaker at a winery in the Zamora region of Spain. Despite having no family ties in the world of wine, the agriculture engineer created history and became the first woman in Spain to achieve the MW title. There are many such underdog stories, where candidates have proved that it is possible to beat the odds.

This year of travel and exploration also taught me about people working in the wine industry and how a common love for the drink transcended every boundary. I encountered several people who went out of their way to help me get a glass of wine to taste. These were people who had nothing to gain if I ever became an MW, but they were generous nonetheless. Bartenders and shop owners in strange cities would send me a complimentary bottle or a glass of wine from a bottle that had been opened for other guests when they found out I was an MW student. I didn't have to explain anything; they just understood my struggle and offered to help in the smallest yet the most significant way possible. I was grateful for every drop of wine that made it to my glass.

Perhaps I should clarify here that when I say 'tasting', I don't mean lying back in an easy chair and sipping wine while soaking in the sun, or partying late into the night at a bar and downing glass after glass of exotic wine.

Tasting wine is different from drinking it. When you taste, you channel all your senses in analysing it, deliberating on each step and deducing from it.

There are four essential steps in wine tasting, and each step can provide clues as to which wine it is, where it comes from, its quality, its style and its commercial potential (that is, where it might succeed in selling).

Step 1 is looking at the wine. Wine must be clear, because cloudiness indicates a fault. The actual colour and how deeply hued it is can point you towards certain grape varieties. For example, Pinot Noir and Nebbiolo produce light-coloured wines, whereas Malbec and Shiraz make deep-coloured wines. White wines go from lemon to gold in colour as they age, whereas red wines fade. A golden hue in white wines can also indicate that the wine has spent some time in an oak barrel. These factors, therefore, provide hints on the grape variety used, the age of the wine and whether it has been oak-aged.

Step 2 is nosing the wine by sniffing it, keeping your nose close to the rim. Swirling it in your glass before sniffing allows the aromas to release and become vivid. Most notable grape varieties have signature aromas; for example, Chardonnay and Pinot Grigio smell of apples and pears, whereas Sauvignon Blanc more aromatically displays notes of grass and guavas. In red wines, aromas of black plums are associated with Merlot and black pepper with Syrah. Now these grape varieties grow across several wine-producing regions where the climate may differ. A cool climate tends to produce lemony, green apple and citrus fruit notes, of the kind that grow in colder countries; whereas warm climates produce riper and sweeter fruit notes of pineapple, melons and mangoes, fruits you find in tropical climates. Then there is the factor of age. You tend to find fresher fruit aromas in young wines and dried fruity notes in wines that have matured gracefully. Thus, analysing the aromas can also provide pointers to which wine it may be, the climate of the region where it was produced and whether or not it is a young wine of a recent vintage.

Step 3 is tasting the wine. Professionals typically take a small sip, let the wine swish around in the mouth, touching all parts of the tongue, perhaps suck in some air to unlock some hidden flavours and then most importantly, spit it out. Spitting wine out is important because wine is an alcoholic drink and it is important to maintain sobriety when tasting in a professional environment. Flavours of wine mostly coincide with the aromas, but the more important element in tasting is making note of the structure of the wine, and by that I mean making observations about its levels of sweetness, acidity, tannins, body, alcohol and finish. All these provide data points. And when you plot these points together, it can lead you to certain types of wine. For example, a dry red wine with tart acidity, grippy tannins, a full-bodied mouthfeel, warming alcohol, flavours of red fruits and a persistent finish points to a Barolo, a classic wine made from the robust Nebbiolo grape variety that grows in the Piedmont region of Italy; whereas a dry red with fresh acidity, low and soft tannins, medium level alcohol, a light-bodied mouthfeel with bubble-gum and bananas flavours and a crisp finish is more typical of a Beaujolais, a young fruity wine made from the Gamay grape variety. Like this, there are many different permutations and combinations across multiple grape varieties and regions where the wines are made.

While most wines are distinctive, there are several overlaps. For example, an off-dry (slightly sweet) white wine could be a Riesling, Chenin Blanc, Pinot Gris or a Gewürztraminer. These are called 'laterals', which refers to wines that have some similar characteristics and can therefore be confused for one another. However, as an MW, you must be able to differentiate and tell one apart from the other by analysing the entire wine rather than being led by overlapping similarities. In the MW exam, even if I felt sure of what the wine was in the first instance, I needed to refrain from simply jumping to a conclusion. For example, an aromatic Sauvignon Blanc from the Marlborough region of New Zealand is what we consider a 'banker wine', which means it is easy to identify and you can cash in on the marks if it appears on the exam. However, for the purpose of demonstrating knowledge, I would first have to argue why it could not be a wine from another region, stating that a wine coming from Stellenbosch in South Africa would have riper peach aromas, whereas a Chilean Sauvignon Blanc would be more herbaceous to taste. The same grape variety from the Loire Valley in France would be grassy but perhaps display some mineral notes due to its cool climate, and display oaky notes if it was coming from the Bordeaux region. This way, a taster's responsibility is to show the examiner their strong knowledge of the grape variety and its expressions from around the world, and that alternatives have been considered and eliminated for logical reasons before concluding what the wine is.

Step 4 is deciding on the quality of the wine. High-quality wines have a better balance of flavours, which linger longer on the palate even after spitting. They have deeper and a wider variety of flavours to offer as compared to simpler wines that are simply limited and may even sometimes lack the finesse, depth and precision of a well-made example. It is also important to consider if the wine has matured elegantly, offering complex notes of earth, tobacco and savoury fruits.

The process of wine tasting allows a taster to appreciate different aspects of wine, and then decide on its style, personality and in what context such a wine would thrive. For example, is this a wine most suitable to be sold in a supermarket at an affordable price or would it be worthy of listing at a fine-dining establishment? But the most important thing to remember is that your conclusion must always be constructive and objective, never pejorative of the wine. Even a two-dollar wine that sells tens of million cases each year is as commercially important as a super-premium collector's wine that has the ability to age for thirty years and is sought-after for its brand status.

The beauty of blind tasting is that it takes away all prejudices and allows you to assess the wine independent of all bias. In a blind tasting, you are told nothing about the wine, including its grape variety, region, producer or price. So tasting wines blind allows for an objective evaluation based on sensory perception rather than relying on preconceived notions about the wine's label, price or origin. If there was ever any truth to the adage 'the proof is in the pudding', nowhere does it apply better than when one is tasting wines blind. The proof is indeed in the glass. That's why they say, *in vino veritas*—in wine, there is truth.

Since there was a lack of mentorship and the availability of many varieties of wines in India, every opportunity to learn came at a heavy cost to me, both financially and personally.

There were days when I would cuddle Rianna while she slept and then sneak out in the dead of night to catch a flight. Sitting in my car, with tranquil streets passing by and barely a soul in sight, I would battle with an existential crisis. *What are you doing with your life, Sonal? Will anything good ever come out of all the labour you are putting in? What if the reward is not worth the pain? What if you are not even rewarded with the title in the end? What will you do with yourself then?*

There were many such rides, as most international flights depart at night. Seasons would change; the restless heat of summer would be relieved by the monsoon. I would watch Mumbai bathe in the rain and then be decked up for the festive season. I would watch Christmas lights replace Diwali lanterns. I would smell the fireworks of New Year's Eve. I would see everyone else whizz past me as I remained in one place, even as my car kept moving. The world around me kept changing ever so gently with each car ride, but that feeling of restlessness was a constant companion, as was a deep longing for normalcy.

I craved the smallest of pleasures of ordinary life—sleeping next to my child, having Sunday brunch with my family, catching a movie with friends on a Friday evening, visiting my parents and eating dal chawal made by my mom or staying in bed the whole day and binge-watching a sitcom for the hundredth time. At that moment, everything else seemed more enticing than what I was doing.

I felt tremendous guilt for not being there for my daughter, parents and husband when they needed me. I wasn't there to hold their hand when they fell sick. I wasn't there to take my parents to meet a grieving relative. I wasn't there to comfort Andrew when he had a bad day at work. I wasn't there to scoop up Rianna in my arms and lull her to sleep when she got tired in the evening. Yes, achievers have no choice but to be self-centred, but it does cause pangs of shame and guilt.

Whenever self-doubt bogged me down, I would ask my mother, 'Mom, do you think I'll become a Master of Wine?'

Always my biggest cheerleader, she would reply without missing a beat, 'Of course you will. Who else, if not you.'

Her cheerful voice and confidence in me would instantly lift my spirits. I would tell myself that if my mom thought I could do it, then I shouldn't have an iota of doubt. Even today, if I face a challenge, I turn to my mother for confidence. It always works!

Eventually, I realised I had to trick myself into loving the process instead of just focusing on success. My obsession with the goal was making me miserable. I needed to enjoy the unique opportunities I was getting to visit wonderful vineyards, talk to winemakers, see the world, make new friends and listen to wonderful stories. How many people get the chance to enjoy a glass of wine at a tapas bar while exchanging a few laughs with strangers or to spend a day under the sun at a scenic vineyard in Italy and soak in the wonders of the European summer? These were memories for a lifetime and were worth savouring, despite being part of a challenging journey.

This realisation dawned on me when I spent one of my birthdays on a train in France, headed from Lyon to Burgundy. I was travelling with a group of fellow MW aspirants who had found out it was my birthday and organised an impromptu celebration. Someone in the group had arranged for a bottle of Crémant de Bourgogne, a sparkling wine made in Burgundy, and another acquaintance had scored tiny plastic cups. I popped the bubbly, and the group toasted me as we drank the wine from those crinkly cups.

I had been missing my family terribly since the morning, but the group's gesture cheered me up. I told myself that while I could have been anywhere that day, the reality was that I was on this train, with people who understood my struggles, drinking a delicious wine. Perhaps it wasn't the best way to celebrate my birthday, but it certainly wasn't the worst, so why not enjoy this moment?

Moments like these also transformed my relationship with wine. People often ask me when I fell in love with wine. As it must be clear, this was not a case of love at first sight. Even when I was sure I wanted to pursue a career in wine and attain the highest qualification in the field, I wasn't head-over-heels in love with the beverage. I had grown to admire it deeply and was passionate about wine communication, but to love it with all my heart—well, that took some time. I cannot point to a single moment when the love for wine crystallised in my heart, but it's a cumulation of the experiences I had in this journey.

For example, I remember my visit to the Royal Tokaj winery in Hungary. That region of Hungary is known for its nobly sweet wines, which are considered some of the best wines in the world, often commanding a super-premium price. The IMW had organised this visit for MW candidates to help broaden the students' perspective of wine, and it certainly broadened mine.

Hungary has a long history of producing wines famous for their unique sweetness, which comes from a special process called 'noble rot'. This natural phenomenon happens when grapes are left on the vine longer, allowing the fungus botrytis also called the noble rot, to develop on the fruits. This infestation causes the grapes to shrivel, thus increasing the concentration of sugar in them. These mould-infected grapes, also known as Aszú berries, are then handpicked and used to produce a delectable sweet yet refreshing wine with rich, honeyed flavours and an incredible depth that makes it stand out.

What makes Tokaji wines truly special is their balance of sweetness and acidity. The yields are quite low so the grapes from one plant can only produce a quarter bottle of wine. Producing Tokaji wines is a labour-intensive process that demands precision, which is passed down from one generation to the next.

Tasting those sweet wines after seeing how they were produced, I started to appreciate the precision and hard work winemakers put into their craft. I couldn't help but marvel at how a single fruit like grape can create so many styles and varieties of a beverage with such diverse aromas and flavours, something no other fruit or grain can do. The same fruit could produce a bone-dry wine with little to no sweetness, but in another region or in a different climate, it could yield decadent sweet wines. Wine can have aromas of fresh fruits like strawberries, bananas, pears, blackcurrants, lemons or mangoes, or of spices like star anise and cinnamon or earthy smells of mushroom and leather from ageing. Basically, the wine smells of everything but grapes. It seems impossible for a single fruit to express so many aromas, and yet, it happens.

I learnt many such fascinating concepts through my wine travels. I remember one winemaker in Italy mentioned to me that the alcohol content in wine doesn't just cause intoxication— it plays a part in giving each wine a unique personality and a bouquet of aromas. Wine is nothing but fermented grape juice in its purest form—winemakers do not add any additional flavouring substances or chemicals. Of course, many decisions are taken by the winemaker during this journey to add more stylistic variations in the wine, to give it more clarity or to make it more stable. But at the end of the day, there is a reason why wine is called the most natural alcoholic drink; this is because winemakers do not add or remove anything from it.

The more I travelled, the more I got to speak to winemakers. And the more wines I tasted, the more I fell in love with this amazing beverage. These interactions and experiences also helped me communicate about wine better; my knowledge of the subject wasn't coming just from books but from directly experiencing the world of wine. Travel was broadening both my mind and my palate.

Another memorable trip was to the Bordeaux region in France— home to some of the most revered wineries in the world, such as Château Margaux, Château Brane-Cantenac, Château Pichon Baron and Château Leoville Barton. As always, I got to drink several fascinating wines on this trip. One of the highlights of this trip for me was our visit to Château Cos d'Estournel, where I was stunned to find that the architecture of the winery closely resembled the pagodas of Asia. The château's founder, Louis Gaspard d'Estournel, was known to have a fondness for India, which is reflected in the château's architecture, as underneath the pagodas is an ornate wooden door guarded by elephants. To see the Indian elephant as the symbol of this esteemed winery, sculpted in stone, wood and shrub across the château's premises, filled my heart with fondness and pride. It was a reminder of India's vast legacy and influence across different continents. India might be discovering the world of wine now, but it had been woven into the history of wine centuries ago by this estate.

During our visit to Bordeaux, for a couple of days we stayed in Sauternes, which produces graceful sweet wines. The amber-coloured wines have aromas of honey, orange marmalade and spices. The producers of Sauternes wines always emphasise it isn't just a dessert wine and can be paired with a range of dishes. While visiting wineries in Sauternes, we were treated to lunches that explored the wine's versatile food compatibility. One of the most popular food pairings was with liver pâté, which is made by grinding pork liver with lard. Liver pâté is a popular French delicacy, so my fellow students were thrilled to try it with exquisite Sauternes wine. As a pescatarian, I hadn't been sure of what kind of food would be available on this visit. So, I had registered for the tour as a vegetarian, and was served dishes like cucumber and cream cheese roulade or fruit-based salads.

As the tour progressed, my friends' reaction changed from 'Ah, pâté' to 'Ooh, pâté, again' and then 'Oh, pâté, again.' By the third day, people would hover over my table, looking wistfully at my plate of fresh veggies and cheeses, and say, 'We want what you have!'

This experience proved that every food and cuisine can be paired with wine if you understand the fundamentals of pairing the two. Many foods suppress certain taste buds on our tongue, momentarily altering our perception. The simplest example of this is drinking orange juice straight after brushing your teeth. The juice tastes sour and bitter because toothpaste contains sodium laureth sulfate, which suppresses the taste buds that detect sweetness. Understanding this interaction between different foods and beverages is the key to wine and food pairing, so that the wine you offer doesn't get overpowered or altered in taste by the food you serve it with. Sour foods, such as tomatoes, vinegar, lemons, enhance the flavours of wine, making it taste richer. Salty foods like salted cod, salted nuts and salt-crusted pretzels and even bread too make a great pairing with wine, especially with high-tannin wines like Shiraz or Malbec, since salt acts as a flavour enhancer and softens the wine's tannins. However, pairing wines with bitter foods like bitter green vegetables or umami foods like eggs or bacon is challenging. Indian dishes can pair with a wide variety of wines, as long as they aren't overly spicy, but this requires another book, which I will write soon.

During these visits, I learnt invaluable lessons from people working in different spheres of the wine industry. Ironically, these people were not MWs themselves, but their wealth of experience and practical knowledge was immense. Come to think of it, an MW learns the most from people who are not MWs themselves! However, every person I interacted with had immense respect for the title and for the students who pursued it. I think the respect was for the determination, focus and dedication that we students put in. Once a person becomes an MW, they earn respect from the industry for the time and effort they invest to further develop the industry.

An MW is meant to be the keeper of knowledge of the wine world. The whole reason for being vessels of knowledge is to share whatever we know with the rest of the world—that's the core virtue of every MW, because knowledge has no power unless it is shared.

Over the six years, I also realised that the wine world is constantly evolving, with innovations in how wine is produced, marketed or accessed, and because of the impact of external factors like climate change on the industry. This meant that even after one became an MW, the learning never stopped.

11

Winner's Mindset

Apart from tasting wines extensively, an important part of the preparation was sitting for mock exams. These exams offer an instant check on a candidate's current status and areas for improvement. However, mock tests were only helpful if they were followed by an insightful session on how a candidate could improve their answers.

Many MWs organised private lectures and mock theory and tasting exams for MW aspirants to give them constructive feedback that could help improve their performance.

Only a very small percentage of people pass the programme in merely three years. Those who pass Stage 2 in the first attempt, as rare as they may be, are considered superhumans. Once, I signed up for a tasting practice with an MW who had passed his exams on the first attempt. The session required me to travel to the British countryside, that too without a smartphone or Google Maps. The challenging travel aside, I was excited about the session as I thought I would finally discover 'the formula' needed to succeed in the tasting exams. But, much to my dismay, the session wasn't as productive as I'd expected. The eureka moment I had imagined never came. This made me realise that people who have failed on their MW journey are perhaps better teachers. After all, failure is a better teacher than success.

The MWs who took multiple attempts to clear the exam could correctly identify where you were going wrong, drawing from their experience.

My dear friend Richard Hemming MW too helped me with my preparation. Richard was a year ahead of me in the programme and had cleared the tasting exam by then. When I reached out to him for help, Richard hosted me at his home for an evening and tasted wines with me, analysing my answers and sharing his insights and suggestions. He taught me how to create laterals for wines similar in style and structure, compare them and present a comprehensive answer.

Then, during one particular seminar hosted by Matthew Stubbs MW, something just clicked. It's like I took a step back while viewing a painting and suddenly the art presented itself in all its glory. He gave me immense clarity on how to write the answers for the tasting papers. He convinced me to stop focusing on getting the wines right, as that wasn't what the exams were about. Instead, he showed me how to get the steps to answer the question right and collect marks for that. Paying heed to his advice, I turned my attention to deducing as much as possible from what was in my glass while writing with authority and providing structured answers. Over the next three months, I solved several past examination papers and I felt I was improving every single time. I believed I had finally cracked the code!

When I walked in to write my tasting exams, I didn't care what wine was poured into my glass, because I would write about it like an MW. A combination of all the travels, tastings, discoveries, failures and relentless practice had given me the winner's mindset. Maybe that's why the programme says that you would earn the title only when you could demonstrate that you are an MW.

I wrote the three tasting papers and passed. That year, I had felt like an MW in my head and that power had transformed into reality. That's the winner's mindset—you go to war knowing you've already won. Once you develop it, you'll always approach your problems confident that you will overcome them. In the moment of success, everything comes together for you—the mindset, along with a little bit of luck, the tremendous adrenalin rush, the absolute focus that puts you into a zone where you see nothing else but your goal. Once the moment passes, you can rarely get into that zone again. Such moments come sparsely in your life. How many people who have scaled Mount Everest will be willing to do it again the minute they return to the base camp? Be it scaling a mountain, winning a battle, acing a competition or emerging the winner in a race, one needs to have a winning mindset.

Now that I look back, the MW journey wasn't just about earning the highest and the most difficult wine title in the world, it also sculpted me into the entrepreneur that I am today. The programme peeled me layer by layer, rid me of my fears and insecurities, made me live through every emotion, tested every skill I possessed and pushed me to throw myself at new challenges without the fear of failure. I am ready for any firsts now; I am not afraid to try.

This mindset has shaped my career as a wine entrepreneur in a country like India, where we have tried many firsts and built a template for others to use. Uncertainty doesn't discourage me; it is just a part and parcel of being a pioneer.

Passing the tasting exam took a huge burden off my chest as I had cleared the most difficult stage of the programme. It gave me a sense of accomplishment and relief as I no longer had to study or run across the world to taste wines with a clock ticking over my head. I wanted to pop champagne and tell the world that I was set to become an MW. But I had enough experience to know that things could still go wrong. I was yet to pass Stage 3, for which I was required to write a 6,000–10,000-word research paper demonstrating my mastery over a topic and contributing to the understanding of the world of wine. The institute advises students to choose a topic that can have future career applications and has not been covered before. The student must then write an application to the IMW explaining why they have chosen their topic. Since students have to do this in just a couple of months after passing Stage 2, some start working on it even before clearing their theory and tasting papers. If the IMW doesn't approve the subject, the student needs to reapply with a different one.

I was clear on the subject of my paper from the start—the Indian market. It was time to finally focus on what I wanted to do once I became an MW. The business aspect of wine has always fascinated me as I wanted to be an entrepreneur. I wanted to empower the trade with one-of-a-kind research on the Indian market and consumers. This research would help wine-trade devise more effective marketing strategies, make better product decisions and strengthen their brand positioning. I believed the institute would approve this topic as no other student had covered the Indian wine market before.

I looked for research or studies that could provide insights into Indian consumer trends. I was especially hoping to find one done by a UK-based company called Wine Intelligence, known for its research on wine markets worldwide. When I went through their website, I found a report on every country, including China, but not on India.

Wine Intelligence is the number one consumer research company in the world of wine, and I realised that if they didn't yet have a report on India, they would surely want one in the coming years. If I could pioneer this research, perhaps they would with me in the future. This paper could become more than just research paper to pass the exam; it could make meaningful contributions to the Indian and international wine community, helping them understand the awareness, attitude and behaviour of urban Indian wine consumers. If I could write a powerful paper that captured the taste, behaviour and preferences of Indian wine drinkers, it could encourage international producers to explore India, to get a head start in a market that was bound to grow, and to navigate it with confidence. Thanks to my work, they wouldn't be walking into alien territory with no understanding of how it worked. This insightful report could also become a potential gateway for wine producers to enter India and, as its author, I could be the one ushering them in. After all, the winner's mindset is also about having the foresight on how every career move shapes your future endeavours.

For my research, I eventually interviewed nearly 900 urban consumers across Mumbai, Delhi, Bengaluru, Pune and Goa, as these territories represented 80 per cent of India's wine consumption market. We targeted high-income earners across four age groups: twenty-five to thirty-four years, thirty-five years to forty-four years, forty-five to fifty-four years and above fifty-five years. All the participants were Indian residents who had consumed wine in the past six months. My survey partner screened and recruited the participants after qualitative exploratory research, often the first step in a longer research project. In this phase, they conducted face-to-face interviews with each respondent. Next, we did pilot research with ten consumers to help us design a questionnaire, based on whether the participants understood the terminology and methodology used. Based on the findings, I wrote a thirty-point questionnaire that was circulated among the participants. Once the survey was done, the raw data landed on my desk.

It took me months to analyse the heaps of data that the survey generated. I not only wanted to interpret the data and state my findings systematically, but also wanted to make recommendations to wine-trade on how to incorporate the findings into product design and marketing strategies. The research demanded my undivided attention, as one misread statistic could undo the whole project. Perhaps the one quality that this leg of the journey equipped me with is the discipline to focus steadily on a project. It wasn't as adventurous as the preparation for the MW exams; instead, it confined me to my study and commanded me to singularly focus on building a compelling narrative around the Indian wine consumer.

The structure of my report was similar to the reports done by Wine Intelligence, corroborated in the awareness, attitudes and usage (AAU) format. Such a research approach is commonly used in marketing and consumer behaviour studies to understand how aware consumers are of a product or service, their attitudes towards it and how they use it. AAU studies often segment the population into different groups based on their awareness, attitudes and usage patterns. This helps identify key consumer demographics and behaviours that can be targeted for creating marketing strategies.

I had deliberately shaped my report like those written by Wine Intelligence, using the same methodology and style of writing as I wanted to use it like a trail that led the organisation to me in the future. I was also fortunate to have a hands-on mentor in Nicholas Paris MW, who went through the paper at different stages and provided excellent feedback.

Once I had submitted my report to the IMW for review, all I could do was wait. This was the last leg of the journey. I felt I was on the verge of achieving my dream, so I used the time after my exams to enjoy my life the way it used to be. I had a dozen ideas, ready to fire as soon as the title came my way. While my fate remained undecided, I enjoyed the company of my daughter and husband. Those few months after submitting my papers were the first in six years when I wasn't packing or unpacking my suitcase. But as the day of the result grew close, that sense of serenity was replaced by apprehension.

Then, on 6 September 2016, the call from Penny Richards came and my life changed. My first day as India's first MW was spent receiving congratulatory calls and messages. Call it optimism or foresight, I had kept a press release ready to announce the news to the world. Finally, the entire world would know what I had been up to for the last six years.

Once I sent out the press release, I sat with my family to go over the lovely messages I had received from people all over the world, including other MWs, my fellow candidates, colleagues and friends. I was thrilled to receive a message from Gérard Basset, the first person in the world to achieve both the MW and Master Sommelier titles, a feat only three other people have replicated ever since. This outpouring of messages from MWs gave me an instant sense of belonging. They made sure I knew I was one of them now.

Another message that moved me came from David Banford, who had given me my first work opportunity as a wine professional in 2008. While I was doing my DipWSET, David Banford and Kris Engle, the founders of the Wine Society of India, had invited us for dinner to their place one night. The conversation naturally turned to my studies and Kris asked, 'So what is your plan, once you finish your diploma, Sonal?'

'I am going to join the Master of Wine programme,' I said.

'That's a very tough programme; not many people pass the exam,' David said, with a hint of concern in his voice.

Before I could respond to his comment, he added, 'You know what, Sonal, you're very talented. You're a great communicator and the DipWSET in itself is a very high qualification. You'll probably be the first Indian to complete that too. Even if you choose not to do the Master of Wine, you'll still have a great career. So keep a Plan B.'

'No, there's no Plan B. Becoming a Master of Wine is not an option. It's the only plan,' I had said then.

I received an email from David on the day I became an MW. By that time, David and Kris had wrapped up the Wine Society of India and moved to London.

'Congratulations! You've done it, Sonal. Kris and I are so proud of you. I remember when I questioned you about your decision to enrol for the programme, you seemed so resolute. As uphill as this task may have been, you have achieved it. So, full marks to you! Sending you love from London.'

Seeing my parents tell everyone about their daughter's feat with a sense of immense pride in their voices was special. A few days later, they presented me with a gift.

'What's this?' I enquired.

'Open the box and find out for yourself,' my father replied.

The box contained pure silver wine glasses. It was such a sweet sentiment, coming from parents who barely knew anything about wine.

'Where did you even find these?' I asked.

'I had to look at several places, but I found them eventually.'

I still have those wine glasses, and they remain one of the most precious gifts I have ever received.

The MW convocation happened a couple of months after the results were announced. The ceremony took place at the ornate Vintners' Hall, founded by Vintners' Company, one of the twelve great city livery companies, which is known to have played a significant role in the foundation of the IMW. Situated on Lower Thames Street in London, Vintners' Hall hosts IMW events, such as its annual reception and awards ceremony, where new MWs are inducted to its membership.

That day, eighteen new members were being welcomed. All the awardees could bring their friends and families to join in the celebration. Andrew proudly accompanied me to the ceremony, and I also invited Richard to join me on my big day.

I spent days thinking about what to wear for the ceremony, veering from a ballgown to a business suit and everything in between. Eventually, I called my mother to help me with this conflict.

'A ballgown would look really fancy and it'll be perfect for the occasion, but a business suit will look more professional,' I said.

'Why don't you wear a saree, Sonal? You're the first person from your country to get this honour, so why not use this opportunity to represent your culture?'

I was thrilled. 'That's a great idea, Mummy. Plus, I'll stand out amidst everyone!'

I chose a bright pastel green cocktail saree in crepe silk. With its elegant silver border, the saree gave a contemporary appeal to the ethnic outfit, making it perfect for the occasion.

The celebration at Vintners' Hall began with a champagne reception. My saree made me stand out that evening and I got a lot of compliments.

We were then ushered into the ceremony, where the names of the 2016 batch of MWs were announced one by one. Soon my name was announced by the master of ceremonies, who then read a passage about my scope of work, ending it with, 'And we are proud to say that Sonal Holland is now a Master of Wine.'

The room erupted with applause as I walked up to the stage to receive my certificate. I wasn't nervous at all, as the feeling of finally being an MW had sunk in by then. Also, I had never been the kind to be intimidated by a stage. If anything, it excited me.

The awardees received a framed certificate making the induction official. Every student who went on the stage to receive their certificate celebrated the moment in their own unique way. Someone did a little jig that had the room in splits, another raised their certificate in the air like a trophy and jabbed their fist in the air. While walking up to the stage to receive my certificate, I wondered how I wanted to celebrate the moment. There was no point embarrassing myself with a dance. Besides, the celebratory gesture had to be a quick one, because I was barely going to be on stage for fifteen seconds.

I decided to do something unusual and took my certificate, turned it around towards myself and kissed it. I was the only one in the room wearing a bright red lipstick, and now my certificate had a personalised stamp to authenticate its ownership. The audience hooted as I turned my lipstick-stained certificate (nicely protected by a glass frame) towards the room for everyone to see. I am sure there were people in the room that night who thought, 'That's so typical of Sonal!' Nonetheless, Richard approved of my shenanigans, as when I came back and sat next to him, he quietly said, 'Well done.'

Well done, indeed.

I cannot be grateful enough to the IMW for devising this authoritative test on knowledge in wines. It has changed my perspective in more ways than one, be it about wine, success, failure, the importance of hard work, the value of smart work and has given me the realisation that true potential only emerges in the face of adversity. This title compels me to put my authority to the best possible use in India. The sense of responsibility it generates motivates me to always put my hundred per cent into every commitment I make, to challenge norms and to forge a path for others so that their journey is not as difficult as mine, as they have someone to guide them. The title stays with me forever, and so does this responsibility.

Andrew and I had reserved a table at a steak restaurant for that evening. After the ceremony was over, we took some of the senior MWs and other people who had helped me in my journey out for dinner. This was a small gesture on my behalf to thank them for mentoring me over the six years. From Caro Maurer MW, Cathy van Zyl MW, Stephen Skelton MW to Sarah Jane Evans MW and, of course, Richard Hemming MW, nearly a dozen people joined us. We drank, ate, laughed, shared anecdotes and spoke at length about each of our MW journeys, something that's inevitable when a bunch of MWs get together.

When I lay in bed that night, fondly gazing at the certificate perched on the dressing table, I asked my husband, 'Andrew, is this the happiest day of my life?'

'No Sonal, the second happiest. The first was when Rianna came home.'

'Probably the third then,' I said. 'Because the second one was when I married you.'

The Face of Indian Wine

Andrew Holland, Sonal's husband

The first time I saw Sonal was when her friend and then co-worker Sharmin briefly introduced her to me in 1999 as a part of the Oberoi sales team. I was regarded as a very difficult client because I would insist on getting everything I was entitled to as part of our deal.

During the Y2K storm, we had taken up several rooms at the Oberoi and I had managed to get a room for $99—a deal that had been closed by her friend before she left. When we were looking through the rooms, we got into an altercation over the pricing. Suddenly, Sonal teared up in front of everyone and I felt concerned. I asked her if she was okay and she said she was, so I left for my office.

When I went back and checked our deal, it turned out that she was right and I called to apologise, saying that I felt bad for making her cry. Eventually, we agreed to have dinner together and that's how we fell in love with each other.

Sonal was a tough negotiator and every deal with her was a battle, where she won more than I did. Even then, she would always ensure that her clients got what they wanted. That quality is something that she has retained over the years.

When the ice between us broke and we began spending more time with each other, I noticed that she had a great sense of humour and was very articulate. I enjoyed being around her, even though she didn't know a thing about football.

In 2007, I met someone from United Breweries for work and during our conversation, I got to know that the company was planning to go into wine. This was the time when Sonal had quit her job at Kelly Services and was looking to give her career a new direction.

That conversation made me think about my days in the UK where I grew up with Jancis Robinson MW educating people about wine in the country. I thought a similar career trajectory would be very good for Sonal because one, she was very articulate; two, she liked to be on stage and communicate with people.

Then, I came across an article about wine by Jancis and immediately took it home. I told Sonal that she should be like Jancis because there were no wine experts in India. Many people proclaimed themselves to be wine experts because they could throw around names of big wine brands but didn't know much about wines. I thought that if Sonal could combine wine knowledge with her skills, she could do very well.

I was confident about Sonal's success from the start because all the Indian wine experts we met were very shallow and overconfident. While I saw this as a great opportunity, I told Sonal that she needed to build her career on solid credentials without any compromise. This meant that she would have to go without an income and live away from home to study. I told her not to worry about all these things and go for the long shot. I assured her that I was going to invest in her.

We looked at a couple of reputed wine schools whose certifications would give Sonal credibility. But once Sonal found out about WSET, her mind was made up and she assertively told me that this was where she wanted to educate herself.

People think of wine as a glamorous profession. But I have known Sonal to spend her days holed up in her room reading book after book on wine before her exams. It is back-breaking work that requires a lot of stamina and passion and the ability to multi-task. Sonal immersed herself in studies, but she also held on to her full-time job at ITC. And when she got back home from work, she would spend time with Rianna. She never compromised on either of the fronts even when everyone around her told her to take it easy.

I invested in Sonal's future because I was confident of two things: first, that she had a great memory; she could read a book and remember every piece of information in it, down to the reference page. I knew that she would be able to clear any theory exam because of that. Second, she had the ability to pick up skills effortlessly. I wasn't sure how she would go about the process of wine tasting, but she took to it from the very start of her education, and then there was nothing to worry about.

I remember when she did her first workshop on wine in Mumbai, I was there in the crowd. When she appeared on stage and started speaking, it was as if she had been doing it for years. People were invested in the workshop, taking notes, asking questions and thoroughly enjoying the conversation. That's when I knew Sonal was meant to be a wine expert.

However, the journey was not an easy one, with all the travelling that she had to do to different countries to taste various styles of wine. It was very difficult for her to leave our baby at home and go abroad. She knew Rianna was in great hands back home as her mother and father had moved in with us to take care of her. But mother's guilt would often get the best of her. All I could do was encourage her to keep her eye on the ball.

I am happy with the way Sonal has shaped her career as an MW. Instead of resting on her laurels, she has used the title to try different things. Not all our ventures have worked out, but Sonal is extremely resilient along with being a great multi-tasker, and these qualities have helped her stay ahead of the curve. My job is to keep asking her about the status of the work. It is Sonal who drives the entire project on her own, not resting till it gets done. She loves the thrill that comes with the kill, and that's why she is so good at negotiations.

There were a couple of people who tried to hire Sonal after she completed her MW, but she had always wanted to start her own business. When things wouldn't work out, Sonal would get apprehensive. Once, she came to me and said that the industry would only respect her when her business started making money. But I disagreed. I told her that the industry would respect her if she launched game-changing initiatives that had a positive impact on the industry. If you can move the needle for the wine industry by doing things that haven't been done before, you'll earn the industry's admiration.

Thereafter, every decision she has made, Sonal has asked herself what kind of impact it would have on the Indian wine industry, be it launching world-class wine awards to bring recognition to wine producers, setting up a consultancy service to help reputed wine producers enter the Indian market or disseminating knowledge to Indian wine consumers through her social media. It feels great when people walk up to me and call me 'Sonal Holland's husband', and I couldn't be prouder of what she has achieved so far.

I want Sonal to be the face of wine for every Indian consumer, both offline and online. As wine continues to become popular in India, I want her to penetrate further into the market and become a household name. I always advise her to stay one step ahead of her contemporaries and just keep aiming high because there is nothing in the world that she cannot achieve.

12

Tasting Success One Sip at a Time

Now that I was an MW, I needed to think about what I was going to do next. I was firm about one thing—I wouldn't sit on my laurels and wait for opportunities to fall into my lap. After all, a Master of Wine is what a Master of Wine does. So, to remain relevant as an MW, I had to make meaningful contributions to the industry. However, I felt I couldn't do this while continuing to work with the ITC hotels. The lure of creative freedom and building something of my own was calling out to me. So, I quit my job.

I was approached by a leading wine producer and a well-established importer to work for them, but I declined politely, because I wanted to build my personal brand.

India was a blank canvas at the time, culturally new to wine, even from a trade perspective. There was a huge potential for many wine-centric initiatives, which were currently missing. This was an opportunity tailor-made for me. The only way to mould India's wine culture according to my vision was to become an entrepreneur. This would give me the creative freedom and autonomy that I sought.

I hadn't taken my foot off the pedal while doing the MW and I didn't do that even after becoming one. Starting in 2016, I tried many different things every year; some of them worked, while others didn't. The first order of business was to revitalise the academy, which had been dormant for three years. Indian wine professionals had finally started associating a WSET certification with better work prospects, and the academy started seeing a consistent footfall of students. The same year, I launched SoHo Wine Club—a community of wine lovers for whom I would host events and organise shipments of wines. But despite a fantastic start, the club failed to attract people and eventually, I had to put it on the back-burner. Any entrepreneur will tell you that an idea may fail to take off because it's not its time to shine. But instead of giving up on it altogether, you simply put it on standby, like I did with the academy, and then bring it back when you feel that the world is ready for it.

Another opportunity lay in the fact that wine occupied a very small percentage of offerings at restaurants, as compared to spirits or beer. There was a general lack of awareness and education on how to construct a wine programme. Sohowines Consulting was launched to help hotels and restaurants improve their wine offerings. We worked single-handedly as wine consultants for restaurants, using a five-pronged approach, which we called the G.R.E.A.T. wine programme (**G**ood quality wines at **R**easonable prices, curating unforgettable **E**xperiences for guests with **A**ttention to detail and **T**raining programmes for staff).

You remember how I had foreseen a collaboration with Wine Intelligence while I was writing my research paper for IMW? The year I became an MW, I got special permission from the IMW to release the findings of my research, *Understanding Awareness, Attitudes and Usage of Wine Among Urban Indian Consumers.* I held a press conference at the Four Seasons hotel in Mumbai, where I invited the trade and media and shared my findings with them. The findings were widely published both domestically and internationally.

And guess what! It caught the attention of Wine Intelligence and they reached out to collaborate with me on conducting comprehensive consumer research on the Indian wine market. The thought and planning behind the paper, including modelling my writing style on that of Wine Intelligence, had paid off. I was the editor of the *India Landscapes* report published in 2018. The wide global distribution of this report further propelled interest in the Indian wine market among international wine producers and exporters. I started receiving emails enquiring about ways to enter the Indian wine market. This led to the birth of our international consulting practice.

Where on one end, the Indian wine industry stood at an inflexion point and was poised for immense growth, at the other end, India's regulatory landscape was complex and decidedly daunting to decipher for international wine producers. Wine, like other alcoholic beverages, is a state subject with every state having its own set of regulations on the production, distribution and retail of wine. The general lack of transparency and uniformity in the tax regime, with differing excise duty and value-added tax (VAT) structures across states, makes the business selling of wines complicated. For instance, a bottle of Tignanello Toscana, an iconic Super Tuscan wine, costs ₹26,950 in Mumbai, ₹24,750 in Goa and ₹19,500 in Bengaluru. The price difference is even more drastic in the twin cities of Delhi and Gurugram, where it costs ₹28,000 and ₹19,900, respectively. Since these cities are just an hour apart, it is no wonder that many consumers from Delhi travel to Gurugram to hand-carry wines across the border.

This complication presented a great opportunity for us, and we expanded the consultancy to help wine brands understand and navigate the Indian wine market. We facilitated introductions with key importers, advised on pricing strategies and also partnered with them on devising an effective marketing strategy to establish them in this unique market. Eventually, we also worked with trade commissions and consular offices of various wine-producing countries and regions to promote their wines through trade tastings and consumer events.

I've carried forward the research presented in the *India Landscapes* report, enlarged upon it and created the *India Wine Insider*—the complete guide on how to enter and win in the Indian wine market.

On the global stage, I was also getting invited to judge international wine competitions like the Concours Mondial de Bruxelles, the Decanter World Wine Awards and the Hong Kong International Wines and Spirits Competition. This gave me a unique opportunity to continue tasting hundreds of wines from all across the world and keeping my palate updated. Such competitions are also a brilliant opportunity to network with like-minded wine professionals and those who are a part of the wine-trade.

I realised that even in the most developed wine markets, wine competitions help consumers learn more about wines that are worth buying, since medals serve as quality cues that empower choices. India at the time had many food awards but none related to wines. I saw this as a great opportunity to launch a wine competition that would enable Indian wine consumers to make better drinking choices.

We named it the India Wine Awards and our processes were aligned with global standards of judging. Our first competition, held at the Sofitel Mumbai in 2017, received over hundred nominations from international and domestic wineries, a testimony to the awards' credibility.

The awards clearly met a need for effective and impactful communication of quality, as with each edition, they have not only expanded, with a consistent rise in the number of nominations, but have also grown in stature, commanding respect for their unbiased and world-class standards of assessment.

While I was working on these initiatives, the Indian wine market was dominated by unorganised wine retail, run by liquor store employees with little to no knowledge about the beverages they were selling. Small dingy wine shops with long queues outside didn't create an inviting environment where consumers could explore a variety of wines. In short, the wine retail scene was unsophisticated and unstructured, thus making consumer experience non-existent.

Around 2018, Foodhall, a premium lifestyle food superstore chain by the Future Group was launched. It offered gourmet products to aspirational urban Indians who had rising incomes and an interest in luxury lifestyles. I was called upon to consult with the group on their wine counters within the Foodhalls. I worked closely with Avni Biyani, Concept Head, Foodhall Future Group and daughter of the main promoter Kishore Biyani to improve the wine offering. Their glitzy new flagship store, spread over three floors was about to launch in Santacruz. It promised to give consumers the ultimate shopping experience, and had a cooking studio and an upmarket Italian dining outlet located within the premises.

Avni discussed with me the opportunity to launch an exclusive wine and beer retail counter within this new Foodhall and wanted me to take the licence and operate the store in my name. I was excited as this would add a new dimension to my entrepreneurial career. Thus was born Vine2Wine, my first venture into wine retail.

Vine2Wine was a pioneering initiative that introduced consumers to clean and air-conditioned wine stores. The modern format enabled a sophisticated buying experience where consumers could browse through the labels at leisure. The stores employed qualified wine professionals, who helped consumers make a more informed choice and encouraged them to try different styles and labels. The integration of wine retail with a food superstore also allowed consumers to integrate the wine buying experience with errands like grocery shopping, thus increasing convenience. Modernised wine retail was an idea that I believed in strongly, and my instincts have been proven right by the success of sophisticated stores like Mansionz in Mumbai, Pune and Bengaluru, Tonique in Hyderabad and Pune, World of Wines in Mumbai, G-Town in Delhi NCR, and Lakeforest Wines in Gurugram in more recent years.

In the midst of all this work and my efforts in several different directions, tragedy struck. In 2018, my father contracted a respiratory disease. His condition deteriorated rapidly, and he was admitted to the intensive care unit at the hospital. My sister and I put our work on hold to be with him and to support our mother.

While I was sitting outside the ICU, my calendar pinged with a reminder that I had committed to hosting a launch party for Fratelli Wine's J'noon collection. Fratelli founder Kapil Sekhri and vintner Jean-Charles Boisset, who had crafted this exclusive collection, were flying to Mumbai for the launch. I was in a conundrum—how could I leave my father, with his condition deteriorating by the day, to go and host an event? How would I even focus on anything else and be myself on stage? I thought I should call Kapil and apologise, saying that I wouldn't be able to do it.

I mentioned this to my mother, who was sitting with me. She was quite firm, 'No Sonal, you can't back out now. Papa would never want you to walk away from a commitment. You must go. Do it for him.'

She was right. Daddy would never want me to back out so close to the event and leave my colleagues in a lurch. So I went home from the hospital, got ready and hosted the launch of J'noon. Around 150 guests turned up at the Four Seasons Hotel and spent a beautiful evening of conversation and wine tasting, loving every moment of it. My role required me to be centre stage, and I put all thoughts of my father out of my mind for that brief duration and ensured I gave it my best.

I wanted to leave the event as soon as it was over, but Kapil and his wife Puja insisted that I stay for dinner. It was then that I told them about my father's condition. 'I need to get back to Mulund as soon as possible, Kapil. My father is in the ICU at Wockhardt Hospital.'

Kapil and Puja were shocked to hear this. 'Why didn't you tell us? You could have opted out and stayed in the hospital with your dad,' Puja said in disbelief.

I shook my head and smiled. 'I had committed to the event, this was an important launch for you all, I couldn't let you down,' I said.

I went back to the hospital at midnight to check on my father. His health had deteriorated beyond hope. I spent the night with my mother in the hospital, feeling numb and praying for a miraculous turnaround. He passed away the next morning.

Losing him so suddenly was a huge shock, but I tried to keep working as a way to cope with the loss. A man with a strong work ethic, my father would be proud of the way I handled my grief and continued working after his demise, even when my heart struggled to cope with this unbearable loss. It is easier to stay motivated when life is kind, but much harder to keep one's chin up and work through adversities.

Between mourning and working I got some time for self-reflection too. I was now in the process of becoming India's first wine influencer, and the consultancies I ran were growing in reach and influence. Yet all this could perhaps have happened even without the MW title. How could I become a significant MW? How could I bring the title and all that it entailed to bear on my work?

I started studying the careers of others who had gained relevance after becoming MWs, such as Jancis Robinson MW, James Suckling MW, Robert Parker MW, and tried to see if I could bring to the Indian market what they had brought to their countries.

I realised these wine professionals were respected because of their contributions to the wine world. For instance, Robert was the first to objectively assess the quality of a wine by introducing a hundred-point scale to score them. This simplified wines for consumers, as they could now easily correlate a high-scoring wine with good taste and quality. Meanwhile, Jancis chose to follow the trade path, adding immense value to the industry by using her background as a writer to pen volumes on wine that became the reference point for every person pursuing a career in this field. She became the master of MWs.

Eventually, I realised that till a point in one's career, an MW needs the institute's backing, but beyond that, the institute needs the individuals. IMW's significance lies in its MWs; its success story, glory and aura are firmly rooted in all the good work that its members do. Only when MWs build successful careers on the foundation of their titles does the institute's relevance grow. The IMW celebrates the success of those who add laurels to their title. I wanted to reach a stage in my career where the institute celebrated my success and proudly endorsed me. To achieve such prominence, the Indian wine market had to flourish first. For that, I had to find initiatives that would help popularise wine.

This meant trying a hundred different things to find my niche, knowing very well that the wine industry in India didn't have as much depth as countries like the UK, France or the US. So, when you don't have depth, you should go for breadth.

The business platforms I had built were starting to pay off and as a result of my efforts, the industry and consumers were steadily reaping the benefits of my expertise.

Yet all of this work was happening in physical spaces— through stores and workshops and publications. The reality of our times is that most people spend a large part of their time online, stuck to their phones, and that is where new trends are created. A change in the Indian consumer's attitude towards wine could not occur without an online push as well. I needed to be on social media.

13

Building a Personal Brand

I had been tinkering with social media since 2014 and in 2020 had reached about 20K followers. During COVID, all my businesses came to a standstill and I got a lot of time to reflect on my career and skill set. My goal, when I started my wine career, was to become India's first Master of Wine. But the journey henceforth had to be about shaping a personal brand that would draw people in and add value to their lives. Working in a niche industry, I had to think hard about what value I could bring. I had engaging communication skills, sufficient knowledge of wine and an understanding of India's developing market. I had a 1.4 billion strong audience that was eager to learn more but didn't even know the basics of wine.

The Indian and global wine communities were on separate tracks. While India was still a nascent market, a vast majority of MWs were working in mature markets where wine was a mainstream drink. I felt my raison d'être had to be different from other wine professionals. Where on one hand the global wine community was discussing the effects of climate change on winemaking and the importance of sustainable vineyard practices, Indian consumers were still grappling with how to open a bottle wine in the first place.

On the social media scene, no one seemed to be simplifying wine for consumers. Instead, most wine professionals were dedicating their time and efforts towards writing academic articles and books that reflected their high qualifications and expertise. Although these books were brilliant for trade professionals, there was still a vacuum in the knowledge suitable for an everyday consumer. Demystifying wine for the consumer, in my view, was still uncharted territory, especially on social media. Wine remained a complicated and intimidating drink.

So my mission became to simplify wine and everything around it—from how to open a bottle of wine and taste it to the best food pairings to busting common myths.

I realised I had two aces up my sleeve—my wine knowledge and the ability to communicate it effectively. My chosen medium had to be videos on social media. My instincts told me I was sitting on the cusp of something amazing.

Due to pandemic-related restrictions, I couldn't call upon a professional team for the shoot, so I did my own make-up and hair, and asked Rianna to shoot the videos on my phone. I started the 'TikTok Wine O'Clock' series before TikTok was banned in India and shared those videos on Instagram. I would explain simple concepts like the difference between red and white wine, how to hold and swirl a wine glass, how to open a bottle of sparkling wine in under sixty seconds, etc. Cooking videos were trending on Instagram so I decided to cook with wine. One of my most popular videos at that time was that of me cooking Spanish flaming prawns with white wine. Many of my followers messaged afterwards asking for the recipe.

Another big trend at that time was that of Instagram Lives. From home workout routines and kitchen tutorials to gaming sessions and music concerts, this became our window to the outside world, a way to connect with each other, a medium for celebrities to interact with their followers and a distraction from the calamity unfolding around us. So I decided to ride the 'Instagram Live' wave and reached out to prominent wine personalities for my video series called 'A Great Glass with Sonal Holland'. Academy Award-winning director, producer and screenwriter Francis Ford Coppola (the man behind the famous *Godfather* film series), Jancis Robinson OBE MW, British actor Dominic West, celebrated vintner Jean-Charles Boisset and chef Gagan Anand, were just some of the distinguished guests that the show hosted. It raised my profile on social media as an influential wine expert. 'How do you know Coppola?' read every third direct message I got after the livestream with the famous director. Now there's a story worth telling.

I met Mr Coppola in 2018 when I was invited to celebrate a hundred and fifty years of Château Lafite Rothschild—one of the world's most celebrated and revered wineries. Château Lafite is one of the only five wine estates listed in the 1855 Grand Cru Classé top tier, also known as Bordeaux First Growths. The invitation had been personally extended by Baron Éric de Rothschild, the president and chairman of the board of directors of Rothschild & Co Concordia SAS, to spend an exceptional evening in the company of selected guests and taste some of the best vintages from the last hundred and fifty years of Château Lafite. Only twelve people had been invited for the celebration and I was the only Indian amongst them.

Mr Rothschild was at the door to receive all the guests. And as if it wasn't surreal enough to be welcomed into such an iconic winery by its chairman, I was thrilled to find that I had been put up at the château, the family home, just two doors away from Mr Rothschild. After the guests enjoyed high tea, Mr Rothschild walked me through the gorgeous Château Lafite estate. He was curious about my career being the only MW in India and listened intently as I told him about my journey.

'I am impressed by your work, Sonal,' he said when I was done. 'We are very pleased to have you here. Thank you for joining us today.'

'I'm the one who should thank you, Mr Rothschild. I feel fortunate to be here,' I replied.

Finally came the evening that I had been looking forward to. When I sat down for dinner, I was surprised to find Mr Coppola seated in front of me and Dominic West on my right. While he was yet to feature in *The Crown*, West was popular for his work in series such as *The Affair* and *The Wire*. Yet, he had no airs of stardom and I thoroughly enjoyed his company over the evening. West didn't claim to be a wine expert but it was clear that he loved his wines.

Mr Coppola, on the other hand, is a seasoned winemaker. His renowned Francis Ford Coppola Winery was acquired by Delicato Family Wines in 2021. However, his family owns and operates the Inglenook Winery in Napa Valley and Oregon's Domaine de Broglie. He regaled us with his wine knowledge and his experiences as a winemaker. Nonetheless, the highlight of the evening had to be the glorious Château Lafite wines we were served. The oldest wine we drank that night was an 1867 Château Lafite, which remains the oldest wine I've ever tasted. I didn't want the magical evening to come to an end, but after the dinner was done and everyone had clicked pictures with everyone, it was time to retire to our rooms.

I decided to sneak out of the château while it was still dark, as I had an early morning flight to catch. I tiptoed around the house, not wanting to wake up my hosts, but to my surprise, I found the kitchen lights on and Mr Rothschild brewing coffee for me.

'You must not leave on an empty stomach,' he said as he handed me a bowl of chopped bananas.

It took me a moment to get over the shock that Mr Rothschild had chopped a banana for me, and it was then that I noticed the other guest sipping coffee in the kitchen.

'I hope you don't mind taking a ride to the airport with me. My flight is the same time as yours,' said Mr Coppola.

Can this get any better! I thought to myself.

Mr Coppola and I chatted for an hour on our way to the airport. We spoke about his childhood, *The Godfather* films and the fame they had earned him. He told me that his first girlfriend was an Indian. I promised to stay in touch as we exchanged email IDs.

I stayed in touch with both Mr Coppola and Dominic West and wrote to them in 2020 inviting them to join me for an Instagram Live. Both of them graciously agreed. People were thrilled to interact with these celebrities during the live streams and were dazzled by the impressive guest list I had managed to curate for 'The Great Glass'.

Due to these collaborations, my followers zoomed to 100K in no time—and that's a significant milestone for any budding content creator.

With pandemic restrictions lifted, my next step was to professionalise my videos and hire a team. At the same time, TikTok was banned in India, so we doubled down on our efforts on Instagram. One of our game-changing strategies was hosting weekly Ask Me Anything sessions with our followers. We would receive hundreds of questions and we found that many of our followers had basic questions, which helped us further shape our content strategy. We also kept a close eye on the comments section of our posts to see people's responses. We found that certain topics received more likes, shares and engagement than others and eventually, these patterns carved a path for our social media journey.

Social media demands immense patience and hard work from content creators. Posting great content was never enough. We have stayed consistent on social media, posting one piece of content every day for the last five years. There were times when the number of followers refused to budge. When this happens, many content creators either give up or succumb to purchasing bots out of desperation. But we never gave in to the pressure and stayed the course. We also continued to evolve as social media changed rapidly. For instance, one of the defining moments in our journey was when Instagram Reels was launched and we realised that the viewer's attention span and preferences had shifted. We shifted from shooting videos in a horizontal format to a vertical format and redesigned the textual, verbal and visual aspects of our content for Reels.

We constantly challenged ourselves. From posting three videos per week, we scaled up our video production and started posting a video every day. This was a humungous task, as it meant more scripts, more shoots and more edits. I had to expand my team for this uphill task, but we wanted to keep our commitment to the audience. People were excited to receive direct wine recommendations from a trusted wine authority as it made purchasing wine pleasurable. Providing authentic content consistently doubled our followers.

We stayed hungry and restless and shifted the goalpost farther; we analysed videos, mostly those of creators from other fields like technology, cuisine and luxury, discussed camera angles, lighting, editing style, etc., and ideated on how to improve our videos accordingly.

In August 2022, our video on how to open a bottle of sparkling wine went viral, receiving eight million views. Up to that point in my career, I had merely been an acclaimed wine professional, but social media success gave me popularity. The combination of my personality, my knowledge of wine and my commitment to adding value and creating a relatable and authentic connection consolidated my personal brand. Building it further required me to constantly push the pedal and put in maximum effort every day, even if the results weren't instantly visible.

From English content, we also diversified into languages like Hindi and Marathi. Our intent was to make wine accessible across all social demographics, thus increasing its appeal and visibility. We didn't stop there; over time, we expanded the scope to include spirits, sake, beer and cocktails. This meant more studies, but more about that later.

The important point to remember is that our strategy always rested on five pillars: consistency in posting, great content strategy, staying committed to the cause, building a community over time and increasingly converting viewers into followers with diligent engagement.

I have always prioritised investing in myself, be it getting the best possible education, upgrading my skills, broadening my experiences or reinventing myself as a wine professional.

Self-belief is integral to building a personal brand because if you don't believe in your potential, you cannot expect others to do so. I bought the domain name sonalholland.com twenty years ago while I was working at Kelly Services. Wine was nowhere on my mind. But even then, I felt that I wanted to do something remarkable with my life and that when that happened, I shouldn't have to struggle to have a domain in my own name. This was how I placed my intent out in the universe and committed to building myself up.

It is important to act quickly on your ideas. I think ideas are like atoms, floating around in the universe, hitting ten different people at once. They never belong to the person who gets them, but to those who act upon them. So, if I don't act on an idea, even if I may be the first person to have thought of it, I have lost my claim to its outcome. One such idea has recently come to fruition.

Just a few months ago, Andrew and I launched our dream project—The Holland House, a French château-style luxury mansion nestled in the valley of Nashik. Spread over 2.5 acres of land, this opulent residential space is an elegant amalgamation of European architecture, modern comforts and Indian hospitality. The five-bedroom villa offers discerning guests an immersive, world-class wine experience with visits to nearby wineries, private lunches and educational tasting tours. The versatile château is a perfect weekend getaway with friends, family and colleagues, allowing guests to explore Nashik's rich cultural heritage and wine-growing legacy while enjoying a peaceful holiday. The Holland House also provides a platform for some of the biggest wineries in India to collaborate and push barriers to create immersive and enriching wine experiences.

As the popularity of wine grew in India, it was evident to me that Nashik would emerge as the capital of wine tourism. If Napa Valley can generate $107 million in tax revenue for residents with 3.7 million visitors in 2023,[11] think of what a country like ours, with a billion-plus population and a thriving economy, can do! Nashik has the potential to become a hundred-million-dollar tourism destination and I didn't want to be on the sidelines when that happened. So I took the idea and ran with it.

[11] 'About Us: Travel Research & Statistics', *Visit Napa Valley*, https://www.visitnapavalley.com/about-us/research/.

Growth is not just about you alone, but about working hand in hand with the industry and its stakeholders. I've always strived to ensure that India's relevance in the wine world continues to grow, be it as a wine producer or consumer market.

To this end, I had been trying to manifest a chance to host Jancis Robinson MW in India for several years. I had requested Jancis to explore India's changing wine culture with me on multiple occasions. Finally, she wrote to me in 2024 and said, 'Sonal, Nick and I are on our way to Bhutan via Delhi.'

The cogs in my brain began turning instantly; this could be the chance I had been waiting for. 'Jancis, you know I have requested you to let me plan a visit. Let's do that now?'

The timing of her visit was going to take a toll on my team because we were set to organise a large trade show in association with Vinexposium, a global leader in organising wine and spirits events, at the same time. My team had been working tirelessly for six months to execute the show and as the date came closer, we were giving our hundred per cent to ensure it was a success. Planning and executing a two-day visit for Jancis was going to be a challenge for us at this point, and she was sensitive to that.

'I know this is a very challenging time for you, but don't worry. You don't have to organise a lot of events for us. We are quite happy to relax on our own,' she told me.

But my mind was already made up. I wasn't going to give her any time to relax. 'Please don't worry about all that. Let me handle it,' I told her and got to work.

Due to Jancis' stature in the world of wine and my undying admiration for her, this was a huge deal for me. I wanted her to witness the growing consumer interest, the evolution of domestically produced wines and the transformation of Indian wine-trade into a proactive entity driving growth. I knew I couldn't waste this opportunity and had to create an action-packed itinerary.

I also wanted to give every relevant trade member in India a chance to meet Jancis. The sommeliers, winemakers and wine producers were the ones working on the ground to build the industry. They would provide Jancis with a different and highly significant perspective of the industry.

We hosted a series of trade and consumer-centric wine-tasting experiences in Mumbai and Delhi. Amongst these was an opulent showcase of the best wines made in India. The 'Navratna' (nine gems) dinner brought together nine of India's top wine producers under one roof to showcase their best wines. Rajeev Samant, founder and CEO, Sula Vineyards; Ipsita Das, managing director, Chandon India; Kiran Patil, owner and director, Reveilo Wines; Amit Uplenchwar, board member and investor, Grover Zampa Vineyards; Vrushal Kedari, winemaker, Fratelli Vineyards; Sanket Gawand, chief winemaker, Vallonne Vineyards; Ashwin Rodrigues, chief winemaker, Good Drop Wine Cellars; Mahesh Awate, winemaker, Big Banyan Wines and Vishal Nagpal, brand representative, Krsma Estates, all graciously accepted our invitation to attend this wine dinner.

Everybody dressed in traditional Indian clothes for the evening and enjoyed wines while the producers spoke about their vintages and vision for wine in India. As I watched these accomplished professionals enjoy a fun-filled evening together, all I saw was an industry that had come together to put their best foot forward in front of the world's greatest wine writer. There was no sense of one-upmanship; all the wine producers and representatives were appreciative of each other's wines. The room was full of laughter, camaraderie and anecdotes; it felt like a family reunion.

At the end of the evening, Jancis' husband, Nick Lander, said to Andrew, 'No one else but Sonal could have pulled this off. She enjoys immense respect and goodwill, and it is palpable in the room. Only she can get everyone in the room together and make one feel a sense of community instead of competition.'

The fact that I can be the glue that brings the entire industry together gives me immense joy. Nothing else can contribute as much to my legacy as these initiatives.

I believe my personal brand is a true projection of the work I do. My goal remains to make meaningful contributions that steer the industry forward.

This brings us to an important aspect of building a personal brand—public relations, or PR. Some people hate it, some love it and others simply don't know how to use it properly to their benefit, but every person who enjoys some amount of fame knows perfectly well that there is no running away from PR.

I hired a PR agency in the early part of my career, and it helped me establish a positive media presence. But soon, I realised that wine was such a niche subject that even my PR agency was struggling to position me effectively. Eventually, I concluded that even if you hire a PR firm, nobody knows your area of expertise, skills and yourself better than you. I had to take the lead.

From journalists to copywriters, whoever reached out to me in those early days depended on me to build the narrative. I had to give them story ideas and set aside time from my schedule to help them write something valuable about the Indian wine industry.

So, I would provide them with a valuable context for their questions. For instance, if an interviewer wanted me to talk about popular red wines in India, I would brief them about the common red wine grape varieties, what kind of red wines Indians like to drink and so on, because this narrative provided an important context to their questions and helped them write a well-rounded and authoritative article. Because I shaped the narrative and contextualised wine for journalists, they could produce something rich and meaningful. This also created a solid recall among journalists of me as a wine expert. While wine has become mainstream today and many food and beverage writers now hold wine qualifications, I still maintain the same practice of investing in an interview so that every write-up is authentic and accurate.

My personality is an integral part of my personal brand. I'm humbled when people compliment me, 'Sonal, your personality is magnetic. How do you do it?' This always amazes me and I never know how to answer it. I remember talking to my sister about this once.

'Had someone complimented me on my glowing skin and asked for a skincare tip, I would have shared it instantly. But how do I explain this?' I wondered.

'Well, you don't share your skincare routine either. I have asked you a million times!' she retorted.

Ignoring the jibe, I said, 'I could say that I meditate for an hour every day ...'

'No one will buy that,' Rimal said, adding, 'but I think I know the answer, Sonal. I think you radiate positivity. You have nurtured a lot of healthy relationships in life and that's where the pull comes from. Today, if you are in any kind of trouble, not just your family and friends, but a lot of people from the wine industry will reach out to help you.'

Rimal was right, I am blessed with fulfilling relationships on both the work and personal fronts, and the credit for that has to go to my parents, because of whom my core is full of love and positivity. That is why I chase happiness with great passion. I commit to building great relationships and I am present in the moment. On festivals like Ganesh Chaturthi, Diwali or Christmas, my house is always decked up for celebrations and I ensure that all my guests are well taken care of. For me, at that moment, nothing is more important than celebrating the festival with my loved ones in the best way possible, and I invest by serving good food to the guests, getting ready for the occasion and ensuring that my house looks great. I spend time doing something I love with great passion and that replenishes my core. Similarly, when I teach a class at the academy, I am a hundred per cent committed in the moment. It doesn't matter how many times I have taught the same course—I always prep before a class to ensure that my teaching matches global standards and that students truly benefit from their time with me. It's all about giving your best to every task at hand.

Building a personal brand is a never-ending exercise because your need to grow more relevant never ends. It's not a one-time investment that will pay returns forever. You'll have to nurture it just like your business, and a great way to do that is to adapt to changing times. If I talk about wine the same way I did ten years ago, my knowledge and observations will be deemed outdated. It's important to upskill and reinvent yourself every time the paradigm shifts.

A Sister's View
Rimal D'Silva, Sonal's sister

Sonal and I are six-and-a-half years apart in age. We have contrasting personalities that were shaped while growing up; Sonal was an extrovert who loved to party, had a large friend circle and could speak on the phone for hours on end, while I loved to hang out with a few close friends and never got the opportunity to use the telephone as it was always occupied by my older sister.

In some ways we were strangers because of the age gap, so a lot of my growing-up years were spent as a fly on the wall, watching Sonal go through a rebellious phase that tested our parents' patience. To their credit, they never let her rebelliousness have a domino effect on my upbringing. I had the freedom to be the person that I wanted to be and was never burdened with unreal expectations or unreasonable dictates to keep me in line.

Our parents never dwelled on the past; they always tackled problems as they came and then moved on with life. No matter how grave our mistakes were, they would never taunt us, verbally or physically abuse us or threaten to disown us. This ensured that our confidence never got affected by our errors and it conditioned us to grow because of our problems. Instead of magnifying our challenges, they would ask us to plan for the future and to stand on our feet.

Most people carry prejudices in their minds about what a girl or a boy can do. But at no point in our lives did our parents make it seem like we were at a disadvantage because we were girls. Thankfully, we have also found partners who respect us and understand that gender is never a limitation. In hindsight, it feels like our upbringing set a benchmark for the kind of people we wanted to attract in our lives.

When Sonal told us about how dissatisfied she was with her career, she was at a point where she was no longer enjoying what she did. She was contemplating whether she should leave or stay with her current job and what she should do next if she walked away from it. I remember telling her that she was on a sinking ship and needed to get off as soon as possible. My parents and I believed that if she wasn't happy with what she was doing and saw no future, then she should leave her job. It worked because she was looking for validation of her thoughts, and the minute she got support from her family, she could quit her job.

When Sonal decided to pursue the Master of Wine title, I didn't know how to react, because it was an alien world for me. But then she told me that there were just four hundred or so MWs in the world and that if she could gain the title, she would be the first one in India to do so. For me, that sealed the deal, because there was no longer any doubt in my mind.

Our relationship as siblings had only evolved after we got married (in the same year!) and had kids and a family of our own to care for. Settling down in our lives was an equaliser that gave us something common to bond over. No matter the age gap or the contrast in your personalities, eventually maturity prevails, and you begin seeing your sibling as your biggest ally in the world.

It is fabulous to see all that Sonal has accomplished after becoming an MW. She was always a dynamic person, but within an organisation, she was confined by its guidelines. When people of her calibre get absolute freedom to expose and express themselves, they get to evolve on their own terms.

Venturing into a new territory like wine and leading with out-of-the-box ideas can be scary, as you have no playbook to follow, but Sonal owned the experience and made it a liberating one by setting a benchmark in the industry. While she is the kind of person who would have gained influence in any field she chose to pursue, this particular industry has amplified her aura manifold as it plays to her strengths.

Sonal's public speaking skills and sense of humour stand head and shoulders above most people's. It is one thing to be knowledgeable, but it is something else to be able to connect the dots and convey your point, no matter who your audience is. If I can make a comparison, then Barack Obama and Shah Rukh Khan are both fantastic orators—they can convince you about anything if you listen to them for fifteen or twenty minutes. I genuinely feel Sonal is just as good, if not better than both of these individuals. It is important for her to have these skills to become successful in the business that she is in so that she can take her enterprise forward.

However, sometimes I feel that she needs to be a little more grounded. Her determination is so strong that she sometimes loses track of reality in the smallest of ways. In moments like these, I tell her to understand what is happening around her and notice the pulse of her surroundings. Having said that, I am truly inspired by her love for life and her ability to put herself out there without fear.

14

Riding the India Growth Wave

Wine has come a long way in India since the time I started my wine journey—from a nascent wine market two decades ago to one of the world's most promising markets today. The Indian wine market has an immense scope of growth for domestic and international wines of every style and at every price point. This exciting transformation is a result of multiple factors, the first being India's rise as a thriving economy. As I write this book, India's GDP is $4 trillion, and hopefully, we will become the third largest economy in the world by 2030, overtaking Japan and Germany. The growth in GDP has led to a surge in Indian household incomes as well. With more money to spend, Indians have developed an affinity for an aspirational lifestyle and all things luxury, from top-of-the-line smartphones and luxury cars to designer handbags and imported skincare products. As a result, India's luxury market is expected to reach $200 billion by 2030, nearly 3.5 times its current size,[12] and India is projected to be termed a developed nation by the year 2047.

---

[12] Pankti Mehta Kadakia, 'Can India become the next China for the luxury market?', *Forbes India*, 22 February 2024, https://www.forbesindia.com/article/lifes/can-india-become-the-next-china-for-the-luxury-market/89583/1.

It's no secret that Indians love to drink! India is the third largest alcobev market by volume in the world, next only to the United States and China. Every year, Indians guzzle six billion litres of alcohol, over half the world's whisky (a staggering 1.5 billion litres) and double that amount of beer.[13] We imported 219 million bottles of whisky in 2023, which was up by 60 per cent from 2021.[14]

A double-digit growth consistently over the past decade makes wine the fastest-growing beverage in the country. Indians are becoming exposed to the wine lifestyle on account of their social networks, international travel, rising disposable incomes and aspirational living. As the demand for luxury products and more spending drives premiumisation across sectors, wine and other alcoholic beverages are the direct beneficiaries of this upward moving trend. Premium vodka, rum, gin and sake, alongside high-quality wines and craft beers, have grown popular too.

Consumers perceive wine to be healthy, see it as a symbol of success and sophistication, and it is socially the most acceptable drink. No other alcoholic beverage enjoys this trilogy of appeal, and it has worked in the favour of wine remarkably.

---

[13] Abhishek Chakraborty, 'At $4.3 Trillion, India's GDP Doubles In 10 Years, Outpaces World With 105% Rise', *NDTV World*, 26 March 2025, https://www.ndtv.com/world-news/at-4-3-trillion-indias-gdp-doubles-in-10-years-outpaces-world-with-105-rise-8010530; Aman Rawat, 'India - The Whiskey Consumption Hub Of The World', *BW Wellbeing*, 3 July 2019, https://www.bwwellbeingworld.com/article/india-the-whiskey-consumption-hub-of-the-world-172710; 'Number Theory: India's liquor sector aims for growth cocktail', *Hindustan Times*, 13 March 2025, https://www.hindustantimes.com/editors-pick/number-theory-indias-liquor-sector-aims-for-growth-cocktail-101741838253985.html.

[14] 'Scotch whisky: India outdrinks France as top buyer by volume', *BBC*, 13 February 2023, https://www.bbc.com/news/world-asia-india-64621887.

Rapid urbanisation and increased exposure to the Western lifestyle through travel and pop culture have further contributed to wine's popularity in India, particularly among the upper middle-class urban consumers. Wine has now earned a mainstream status, and it is widely served at occasions like weddings, house parties and corporate events and in casual dining along with whisky, beer, gin and vodka.

Today's wine drinker is an educated, well-earning urban dweller, well-versed in the Western wine culture, aspiring to integrate it seamlessly into their lifestyle. Young consumers are an important demographic that cannot be ignored. India is one of the youngest countries in the world, with over 500 million people aged between twenty-one and thirty-five years of age. The younger generation in India is all about experimenting with different kinds of drinks and paying more for better quality. They aren't intimidated by wine, are eager to explore different styles and are willing to learn more about the beverage. Wine also remains popular among the seasoned wine elite—the self-proclaimed wine connoisseurs who are wealthy, well-travelled and have some knowledge about wines. These early adopters of the drink are currently experimenting with newer brands and want to learn more about different wine regions and grape varieties.

Women represent an important demographic for wine consumption in India as they are choosing wine for being a softer, healthier option as well as for its aura of elegance. Research shows that women, in general, feel less inhibited and face less criticism when drinking wine in front of their family members. In a society that has traditionally lived in joint families and encouraged only male drinking, women drinking wine at restaurants, bars and at home is a huge opportunity and a real game changer for the industry. In a way, wine has democratised drinking for women in India, allowing them to join their male counterparts in enjoying a drink. This movement is now reaching smaller cities; with the exposure to urban culture and the arrival of luxury dining options, women finally have the liberty to experience wine regularly.

Purchase trends show that still wines make for just over half of the wines consumed.[15] Out of every ten bottles consumed in India, seven are Indian labels and the rest are imported. Indian wines lead consumption due to easier availability, competitive pricing and a vigorous push in the trade with discounts and offers. Indian consumers generally start their wine journey with domestic labels. As their palates seek newer tastes over time, they tend to explore imported wines of different styles.

Wine in India represents a new way of living. Even the government has a softer view towards wine as a low-alcohol beverage as opposed to hard spirits, and policies around wine continue to be progressive. In 2022, India signed the Economic Cooperation and Trade Agreement (ECTA) with Australia, which significantly brought down the import duty on wine to 75 per cent from 250 per cent, which will be further slashed to 25 per cent over the next ten years. While this book is being written, more such agreements are being negotiated with the UK, the European Union and the US. This impressive drop in duties is a sign of changing times for the Indian wine market. This, along with growing consumer interest in imported wines, has given immense confidence to international producers who want to explore this new and exciting territory.

Two of India's largest wine producers, Sula Vineyards and Fratelli Wines, went public and got listed, clearly showing that

[15] India Wine Insider 2024 Report, https://learn.sonalholland.com/IWIReport2024.

investors, both Indian and foreign, are expecting strong growth from the Indian wine industry. Sula Vineyards also claims to be among the most visited wineries in the world and welcomed over 350,000 visitors in 2024, directly pointing to growing enthusiasm for wine and its lifestyle among Indians.[16]

Today, nearly 70 per cent of all wines sold in India are sold through retail shops while the remaining 30 per cent are sold through licensed premises like bars, restaurants and clubs. The primitive retail scene in India, which at one time included small dingy wine shops, is fast evolving with the emergence of sophisticated boutique experiential stores where consumers can leisurely explore wines from around the world. Modernisation of retail is fast changing the way wine is accessed in the country.

The availability of wine in urban spaces is about to witness yet another transformation. The states of New Delhi, Karnataka, Haryana, Punjab, Tamil Nadu, Goa and Kerala may soon permit home delivery of low-alcohol beverages like wine and beer via e-commerce platforms such as Swiggy, Zomato and BigBasket, with state-level policy amendments in the pipeline.[17] The initiative will make such beverages instantly available to a growing population that engages in recreational drinking along with meals.

The rest of the country too is fast catching up, with wine making inroads into tier-2 and tier-3 cities. The hospitality sector is projected to attract over 2.3 billion dollars in investments

---

[16] 'Great Wine Lives: Rajeev Samant of Sula Vineyards', *The Wine Conversation*, https://www.wine-conversation.com/conversations/great-wine-lives-rajeev-sament.

[17] 'Home delivery of alcohol through Swiggy, BigBasket, Zomato and Blinkit soon?', *Hindustan Times*, 17 July 2024, https://www.hindustantimes.com/business/home-delivery-of-liquor-through-swiggy-bigbasket-and-zomato-soon-101721104474800.html.

over the next five years, adding thousands more room keys to their inventory.[18] This hospitality boom is not just limited to megacities like Mumbai, Delhi or Bengaluru, but will also be evident in smaller cities like Indore, Bhubaneshwar, Manali, Amritsar and Lucknow.

This growth across all sectors of the economy creates the need for qualified F&B professionals working in hotels, retail and trade.

In its sixteenth year now, our academy has created a cadre of over 10,000 trained wine professionals and knowledgeable consumers in India. It has successfully made inroads into smaller cities and towns so that a diverse demographic can access world-class wine education.

Through the academy, we have also launched community-driven initiatives. My struggles as a student and an entrepreneur opened my eyes to the challenges faced by wine industry professionals and students in India. So, in 2023, we launched a one-of-its-kind community via our academy, which connects students to established Indian wine professionals so that they can seek mentorship and find promising job opportunities. By broadcasting job openings, we help our students advance their careers. With nearly 500 members, this thriving community has evolved into a strong wine and hospitality industry support system.

The community programme has also exposed a glaring gap in gender representation within the Indian wine industry. While the number of women working across the wine industry has been

---

[18] 'Investments in Indian hospitality to exceed USD 2.3 billion over the next 2-5 years: CBRE Report', The Hindustan Times, 13 May 2023, https://hospitality.economictimes.indiatimes.com/news/hotels/investments-into-indian-hospitality-to-exceed-usd-2-3-billion-over-the-next-2-5-years-cbre-report/100302059

on the rise, this number needs to grow further. Since women make up 50 per cent of wine consumers in India, they deserve equal representation in the industry so that their preferences are always considered.

To further this cause, the academy has partnered with WSET to launch the Women in Wine: Innovation & Leadership Scholarship programme to provide pivotal educational opportunities and support to women in wine or who aspire to do so and help promote greater diversity. We have offered scholarships worth ₹12 lakh to budding women professionals in the industry. From 150 applications, we selected fifteen winners who received admission to the WSET Level 2 Award in Wines course at the academy, along with mentoring from some of the top industry professionals. Of these, five women who secured top marks in Level 2 were further awarded a scholarship for the WSET Level 3 Award in Wines. The academy hopes this initiative will improve the job prospects of talented women professionals while providing them with guidance and mentorship from top leaders.

We have also recognised that the change in the landscape of the Indian alcobev industry goes beyond wine. The industry now demands qualified professionals across different spheres and thus, we have brought spirits, sake and beer under the academy's scope. In 2024, I completed my Level 3 certifications in spirits and sake from WSET School in London to bring the institute's sake and spirits courses to our academy. We became the first in the country to launch WSET's beer course later in the same year. In the process, I became the country's most qualified alcobev professional. Learning must never stop, and I practise this as much as I advise it to budding alcobev professionals.

Improving the portfolio of imported wines in India over the past eight years, Sohowines Consulting has worked with large wine groups, regional trade bodies and governments of countries like Australia, US, Italy, Chile and Argentina among others. The consultancy has created awareness, education and business opportunities for imported wines through diverse consumer and trade initiatives. Meanwhile, we have revived the SoHo Wine Club as SoHo Wines, a consumer community platform, through which we organise experiential events like luxury wine-paired dinners, themed wine tastings, networking soirees and wine tastings all year round. From the curious novice to the affluent well-heeled connoisseur, our experience-driven events and masterclasses help make wines and spirits approachable and enjoyable. It is such a joy and privilege to be working with leading corporate houses, financial institutions, the Young Presidents' Organization, the Entrepreneurs' Organization, top luxury restaurants and hotels to curate memorable events across multiple cities in India.

As our work broadens its horizons to embrace spirits and sake, our tasting competition too has expanded its scope. Now known as the India Wines and Spirits Award, the competition received a record-breaking 650 nominations across different categories for its latest edition in 2024. Over 320 winning labels were recognised and celebrated at a dazzling awards ceremony attended by more than 300 members of the trade, hospitality and media industries. The gala awards followed by dinner was hosted at the state-of-the-art Jio World Convention Centre in Mumbai. We have published the winners list of this year's competition in a chic guidebook that is widely distributed among consumers and hotel managers to help them make informed and exciting choices in beverages.

Who would have thought that one of the most followed social media pages in the world for wine and beverage education would be from India? Yes, it's true! We are proud to receive the love and support of over a million followers on Instagram alone. There is enormous curiosity and thirst for wine and spirits knowledge in India. Understanding of alcobev drinks is still at a preliminary stage, but we get lots of questions around how to enjoy them, their lifestyle and etiquette, best brands to buy and how to be the perfect host. India has over 1.2 billion users of mobile phones of which over 600 million use smartphones; with infinite potential for growth, we are only just getting started.

Our videos also disrupt the critical narrative around alcohol drinking, endorsing moderate consumption and a healthy lifestyle. We have inspired several women and young drinkers to subvert cultural inhibitions and enjoy their drinks with confidence.

Gaining a deeper understanding of the market, a better appreciation for its nuances, developing a strong nexus with its important stakeholders and promoting awareness and education have helped us build a business that is at the forefront of driving the wine revolution in India. As the industry expands and wine is desired by a wider spectrum of consumers, we continue to review the opportunities that exist within India with a fresh pair of lenses, every day.

15

Woman in a Man's World

Being a woman has always been my strength, and I have never seen it as a challenge or a disadvantage that has kept me from growing in my field. That said, I work relentlessly to ensure that I live my personal and professional life to the fullest. The universe has blessed me with a loving family and professional success, and I refuse to take any aspect of my life for granted.

Women often ask me how I maintain work–life balance. The truth is, it is hard to divide time equally between work and personal life on a daily basis. Former Pepsico CEO Indra Nooyi had once famously said this:

> I don't think women can have it all. I just don't think so. We pretend we have it all. We pretend we can have it all. My husband and I have been married for 34 years. And we have two daughters. And every day you have to decide whether you are going to be a wife or a mother, in fact, many times during the day you have to make those decisions. And you have to co-opt a lot of people to help you. We co-opted our families to help us. We plan our lives meticulously so we can be decent parents. But if you ask our daughters, I'm not sure they will say that I've been a good mom. I'm not sure. And I try all kinds of coping mechanisms.[19]

---

[19] Moira Forbes, 'Pepsico CEO Indra Nooyi On Why Women Can't Have It All', *Forbes*, 3 July 2014, https://www.forbes.com/sites/moiraforbes/2014/07/03/power-woman-indra-nooyi-on-why-women-cant-have-it-all/.

Her statement resonates with me so much, because every single day I have to choose between being a wife and a mother and being an entrepreneur. All I can tell women in my shoes is that it gets easier as your children grow older. It also helps if you manage expectations from the start, are kinder to yourself and create a support system around you that makes life easier and these struggles bearable. Also, pick your battles wisely. No two days in our lives are alike, so adjust your focus daily, depending on the challenges that await you. Some days I am judging international wine competitions, on others I am hosting high-end dinners for an organisation or teaching a course at the academy. No matter what I do, I commit to it fully, giving it my complete focus. And this applies when I spend time with my family too.

I want my home to look beautiful; I know which faucet needs to be repaired or if the coffee table needs a fresh coat of varnish. If we are hosting a party, I will go over the menu and ensure that the guests never run out of aperitifs and that there's no shortage of glassware. I want to be there by my husband's side when he has social commitments; I clear my schedule for Rianna's annual day or parent–teacher meetings. I keep regular salon appointments to turn up well-presented each time, even if it is for a regular workday at the office, a family gathering or a coffee date with my friends. Even if I can't do everything myself, I delegate and ensure that the work gets done.

That's why, just like a superwoman needs her cape, a woman leader needs a cohort of supporters who enable her to lead the charge fearlessly. It can include moms, wives, husbands, fathers, brothers, sisters, colleagues or friends who assure you that your home or work will not fall apart even if you focus your energies elsewhere. I think every pioneer's recollection of their journey is incomplete unless they talk about their support system and acknowledge how its existence allowed them to dare and dream big.

It was only because I could leave my daughter in my mother's expert hands that I could be away from home for weeks at a stretch. My parents would pack their bags and hold the fort at home whenever I was away for my studies. I cannot be grateful enough for the unconditional love and support that they showered on me throughout my life, putting me on the path to success in every aspect of life from an early age.

I have written extensively about the influence Andrew has had on my life. As a husband, he has been equally invested in my success and always holds me to high standards. Sometimes, this tough love does rob me of joy. A few months ago, I took a day off from work to relax at home after a hectic week. Just as I sat down with a steaming cup of tea, I got a call from Andrew, who was away from home on a work trip.

'How come you are at home at this time of day? Didn't you go to the office?' he asked.

'I took a day off, Andrew. I'm tired.'

'Oh, taking it easy now, are we?' he quipped.

His response was enough for me to feel guilty. I quickly gulped my tea and headed to the office.

I would advise women to marry men who fuel their fire and support their vision and never become a hindrance to their growth. Or else don't marry at all. There is no in-between for us, women. I chose a partner who is my biggest fan and wants to see me win and will always have my back.

Not just your husband though—make sure the other men in your life believe in you and are not intimidated by your strengths. The men in my life just bring a different kind of energy that creates a balancing effect. My father guided me as a headstrong youngster and put me on the right path, while my husband anchors my impatience with his calm demeanour.

I surround myself with men who want to co-create my success; hence, I never have to fret over naysayers. Of course, when a confrontation is unavoidable, you need to take a stand, but every woman leader must accept that sometimes, it is better to walk away gracefully and let your work speak for you.

As a woman leader in a male-dominated industry, I am often the only woman at the table or on a podium. I am never conscious of it unless others point it out. Honestly, I'm never bothered by the number of men around me. Once you have built authority in a domain and shown leadership in your career, you enjoy a certain stature in the industry where people know they cannot cross a certain line with you.

However, I didn't enjoy this stature at the beginning of my career, and sexism was the subtext in a lot of conversations I had with men in positions of influence.

'Why do you have to work so hard, darling? You are well-off, just enjoy yourself.' I remember swallowing my pride as a budding wine professional when an established name in the industry threw this gem my way.

'Don't worry about the presentation, darling, just wear your solitaires and come, I'll take care of the rest,' a colleague in the hotel industry once remarked when I approached him to discuss an upcoming meeting.

'Isn't your husband giving you enough pocket money? Why do you need to work?' said one gentleman, when I briefly dabbled in a new business that may have threatened his business.

Even today, many assume Andrew puts money into my business to keep it afloat. But it couldn't be farther from the truth. I can proudly say that all of my businesses are self-sustaining. Taking failures and successes equally well has only increased my risk appetite, and I can confidently take bold decisions for any of my businesses.

No matter how qualified or accomplished they are, women leaders cannot escape sexism. But we have to feel secure in our careers and not feel the need to address it constantly. I don't feel compelled to change a guy's opinion about me or my business. I refuse to constantly be an angry woman who must pick every battle that comes her way—that does nothing but deplete my energy. My focus is always on giving back something good to the industry and, while it's tempting to give it back to all the mansplainers, it is an exhausting task. I would rather use my time to groom other women into leadership roles so that they can pick a few of the battles that I've left untouched. I am blessed with the opportunity to help other women build their careers. Women make up nearly 70 per cent of employees at SoHo Wines, and nearly half of our followers on social media are women. It is not as if I have intentionally hired more women or curated my social media following gender-wise. I may attract more women professionals because they feel the organisation has a safe and progressive work environment that encourages professional and personal growth. On the social media front, I constantly get messages from women telling me how refreshing and inspiring it is to see a woman pursuing her dreams with such knowledge and authority.

In recent years, I have actively looked at how I can fuel the fire for women professionals who don't work with me. I have launched initiatives like Women in Wine, and spoken at women forums like Ladies Who Lead and SheThePeople.TV, which has expanded my reach beyond the wine industry. This way, I hope to inspire women working across different spheres to keep powering through the challenges they face in their professional growth.

Speaking to women from different walks of life and reflecting on my journey over the years has also allowed me to see the internal factors that keep women from realising their potential. First, women are bound by too many fears, which I think stems from their conditioning since childhood. I know every woman can't achieve absolute freedom, but they can push the limits and break the cycle of patriarchal policing for the next generation.

Second, women need to replenish their core. Women are expected to make sacrifices for their families and put their priorities on the back burner. If women don't want to continue giving joylessly, then they need to master the art of chasing happiness. And you do not need to make dramatic gestures of self care to make this happen. Simple acts like getting your nails done, buying a new dress, calling up a long-lost friend for a quick conversation or stepping out with your sister for a movie are all acts of kindness towards yourself that can fill your life with joy. And when you feel replete with happiness, the act of giving will bring you joy instead of seeming like a duty. I pursue happiness like my life depends on it.

'The galaxy is the limit ...'
Sharmin Photographer, Sonal's childhood friend

Sonal and I became friends when we were studying at St. Agnes' High School in Byculla. We both shared a love for dramatics and extra-curricular activities and met while participating in a school play. During the rehearsals, I realised that we were quite similar— loud, unafraid, frank and passionate about what we do. As a result, we connected instantly and have been friends for thirty-seven years.

Sonal has had an extraordinary journey with extreme highs and lows in her life. She has done things that I wouldn't even dare dream of doing, and not all of them were great! She is one of those people who invariably bounce back to land on their feet, and that has kept her going through all the struggles. She has this innate confidence where no matter what she does, she eventually gets it right, even if it's not easy. When she does get it right, the success is ridiculously high, and that's what makes her so special.

This also played an important role while she was doing her MW because it was a really difficult time for her. She had to study a lot and Rianna was still a toddler. On one end, she wanted this badly, but on the other end, she realised what a toll it was taking on her family and herself. I have known Sonal to be a hard-working person, but I don't think she has ever worked harder on anything than her wine education and eventually, she persevered.

The only thing I don't like about Sonal is that she often spaces out. There are moments when you are talking to her but she will go off on a tangent. I can see that she is listening, but she's just not there! She has switched off. It's quite endearing, but it drives a lot of us who are close to her mad. But that's just how she is.

Sonal will never achieve success at the cost of doing something negative; that's how much she values her roots and her parents.

Her extraordinary value system has never let her down in the past and it will never let her down in the future.

For Sonal, it's not about the sky being the limit. For her, the galaxy is the limit.

Life Comes Full Circle

Last year, 2024, proved to be the year when life came full circle for me in more ways than one. In February, I was honoured with the Achiever's Award at the Platinum Jubilee celebration of my alma mater, IHM Mumbai. This was the first time that the institute felicitated its alumni of the last seventy-five years. More than 800 people, including senior leaders and stalwarts of the Indian hospitality industry, alumni, students and staff members attended the celebration. Some other notable alumni who were felicitated at this grand ceremony included Param Kanampilly, chairman and MD, Concept Hospitality; actor Karan Singh Grover; Kainaz Messman, founder, Theobroma; India's first female bartender Shatbhi Basu and Sheila Vasan Singla, independent director, Chrysalis.

I went to IHM at a crucial juncture in my life, when I had been thrown out of college for poor attendance. Had my father not filled out the hotel management entrance exam form, my life would have taken a different path that wouldn't have led me to Andrew or to the MW title. I changed my perspective towards life when I joined IHM, and it rewarded my enthusiasm and sincerity. My father wasn't there to witness this moment, but I am sure he proudly watched me receive the honour from heaven.

I had barely gotten over my sense of accomplishment on receiving this award that I got another fantastic news: I had been chosen for the Outstanding Alumni Award 2024 by WSET in partnership with JancisRobinson.com. The award recognised alumni who made exceptional contributions to creating positive change within the global drinks community. I was chosen among twenty-seven candidates across fifteen countries for putting India on the global wine map.

My life's trajectory changed forever when Andrew handed over the newspaper carrying Jancis' article in 2007 and the WSET became the first step on the tall ladder of wine education. Both Jancis and the WSET played a crucial role in shaping my career as a wine and beverage professional, and they continue to do so even today. While Jancis continues to inspire me, with her never-ending enthusiasm for writing about wine, the WSET has been the institute that has forged the path for my wine career.

The ceremony was held on 23 April 2024 at Guildhall in London. It was an emotional moment for me. When I started this journey, I never thought my work would be recognised so significantly by the institute one day. All I ever wanted to do was to make a positive contribution to the world of wine. But life finds a way to surpass your imagination.

When I reached Guildhall, I was stunned by the scale of the event. The 600-year-old Gothic structure is known for its imposing presence, but that night it was pulsating with joy and enthusiasm. I was asked to deliver a speech, but I had never imagined standing in front of a crowd of nearly a thousand people, that too at such a majestic venue.

'Of course you can do it, Sonal! If not you, then who?' I remembered my mother's encouraging words.

The hall erupted with applause as I walked on stage. To receive the award from Jancis in front of so many distinguished guests and students filled my heart with gratitude.

The communicator in me took over the minute I stepped behind the mic to deliver my speech to hundreds of newly minted WSET Diploma students who had received their certifications the same day. Seventeen years had passed since my first seminar at a Mumbai restaurant, where I had mustered up the courage to sound like a seasoned wine professional before a group of women. And now here I was, the seasoned professional I had always aspired to be.

In my speech, I wanted to offer advice that I wish I had received at different junctures in my career. Now that I could see my life in hindsight, these were words I wished I could say to my younger self.

'First, your journey to success isn't reaching its conclusion— it's only just beginning. Now is when the real effort starts. Your focus should be on creating meaningful impact because true success and recognition come from the value you bring to others. Knowledge alone holds little weight unless it serves a greater purpose. Identify your unique strengths and combine them with your expertise to contribute positively—whether in your community, industry or on a global scale. It's not just about what you know, but how you use it to make a lasting difference.'

'Second, take action on your ideas, because no one is remembered for the things they only imagined but never pursued. I see ideas as free-floating energy, circling the world and landing in multiple minds simultaneously. An idea doesn't belong to the one who merely thinks of it first, but to the one who takes the initiative and brings it to life. If you hesitate, someone else will seize the opportunity, leaving you with the regret of inaction. If you're uncertain about your path, don't shy away from experimenting with different possibilities. Some ideas may not work out, but others will take flight, leading you towards your true purpose. In time, your ideas will shape your journey and reveal where you truly belong.'

'Third, invest in yourself, as it pays the highest rate of return. Prioritise expanding your knowledge, sharpening your skills, broadening your experiences and refining how you present yourself to the world. You are your greatest asset—so never cut corners on your path to excellence. Show up prepared, polished and confident, because the world takes notice of those who bring their best selves forward. Success begins with how you invest in yourself today.'

Another special recognition that came just a month after the Outstanding Alumni Award 2024 as I was named the winner of the Gérard Basset Prize 'Ambassador of the Year' at the Global Wine Travel Awards 2023–2024 for my efforts to give the Indian wine industry strong visibility on the global scene. A nurturing mentor and a kind and generous person, Gérard has set the bar high for wine professionals all over the world. His humble nature, despite the massive scope of his achievements, is something that has always inspired me. To receive an award that carries the name of such a stalwart from the wine industry was an honour.

All the accolades I have won are a reminder that success is a responsibility and I must keep marching forward, believing in my dreams and contributing positively to the world of wine. There's a lot more work left to be done. I am looking forward to the day when wine assumes a place of pride in the Indian alcobev market, when people gain a deeper understanding and appreciation for the beverage, with me as a valuable contributor.

So, one circle completes, and another one begins. I am excited to see what the future holds. As I navigate India's growth story, I want to be in the driver's seat of game-changing initiatives that will propel India's wine and beverage industry to the next level. And as I raise my glass to the road ahead, I know this is only the beginning—because being one in a billion isn't just about breaking barriers; it's about building a future worth toasting to. Cheers!

Acknowledgements

This memoir would not have been possible without the unwavering support of those who have walked this path with me. To each of you who has inspired, challenged and uplifted me—this is my moment to raise a glass in your honour.

I am deeply grateful to the Institute of Masters of Wine for fostering a global community of the most knowledgeable and dedicated wine professionals. Its exacting standards and expansive vision have profoundly shaped my understanding and appreciation of wine, and its business at large. I also extend my sincere thanks to the Wine & Spirit Education Trust, where the foundation of my formal wine education was laid, sparking a lifelong pursuit of learning and discovery.

My educational journey was first ignited by Jancis Robinson MW, whose work and passion continue to be a source of lasting inspiration. Along the way, I was fortunate to form a cherished friendship with Richard Hemming MW—my closest companion in the wine world—whose camaraderie and shared escapades brought laughter and lightness to even the most challenging moments.

I consider myself incredibly fortunate to have found a home in publishing with such ease, and this transition would not have been possible without the steadfast encouragement of Karthika VK, Publisher at Westland Books, and Aurodeep Mukherjee, my Commissioning Editor. Their guidance and belief in this project ensured I remained true to the book's vision—and the deadlines.

I must also thank my remarkable team, who kept the wheels turning at work while I stepped back to dive into memories and string together stories. Special gratitude goes to our Head of Content, Yamini Pustake Bhalerao, who became a trusted colleague and a treasured companion on this journey of reflection and storytelling.

On the personal front, my mother, Rekha Chandole, and my sister, Rimal D'Silva, are the twin pillars of my life. One offers unconditional love; the other, unstoppable cheerleading. While I was away chasing deadlines and dreams, they held the fort at home with grace and strength, ensuring that Rianna never missed her mother's presence. Though my father is no longer with us, his presence remains the steady drumbeat beneath all my accomplishments and the quiet strength behind so much of who I am today.

To Charlotte and Chris Holland—thank you for showing me that becoming a stepmom could be not just meaningful, but genuinely cool. You've added depth and joy to my life in ways I never expected.

And finally, to Andrew and Rianna—my heart belongs to you both. Andrew, you saw my potential long before I had the courage to claim it. You cheered, cajoled and, when necessary, challenged me forward. You have supported me through every high and low, and have truly been the wind beneath my wings. As for my darling daughter Rianna, who lived every moment of the MW journey with me—you have been endlessly patient and loving. Your bright smile and warm hugs light up my world every single day. Being your mother shall forever be my greatest honour and pride.

With my young parents

The centre of my parents' universe

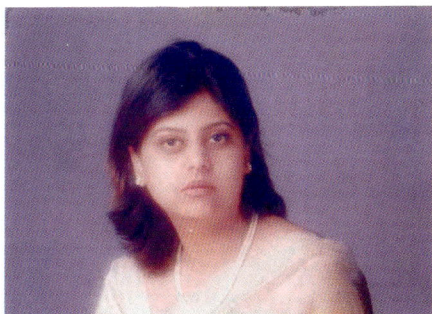
Oberoi days

Tying the knot, Indian style

Studies and travel: A visit to the
Napa Valley, California

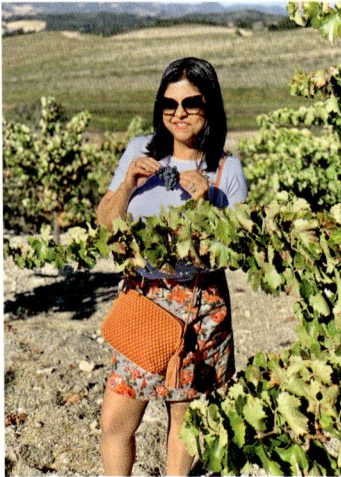
Sunkissed grapes on a vine
in a Californian vineyard

With a selection of Californian
wines in Napa Valley

Inside the cellars of Château Margaux, surrounded by barrels

Baby Rianna comes home

The MW journey continues: With Penny Richards and Richard Hemming MW

Meetings along the way: With legendary film-maker and wine
enthusiast Francis Ford Coppola

Having dinner with actor Dominic
West at Château Lafite

India's first Master of Wine!

With the 2016 batch of newly minted Masters of Wine

The many activities in the aftermath: Judging at the Decanter Asia Wine Awards

Leading a talk at an IMW Seminar

Stalwarts of the Indian wine industry: With the late Kapil Sekhri, Director of Fratelli Wines

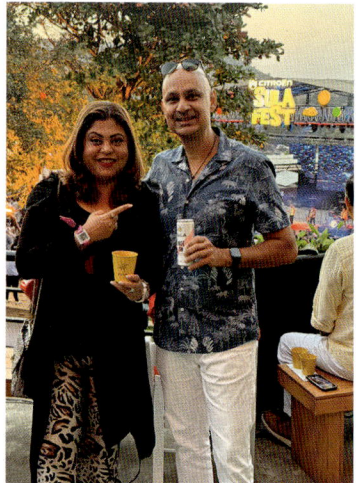

Stalwarts of the Indian wine industry: With Rajeev Samant, Founder and CEO of Sula Wines

A stalwart from the F&B industry: With Australian chef and former Masterchef Judge Gary Mehigan at an event

Building up the wine industry in the country:
India Wine Awards 2017

Vine2Wine: a collective of modern, sophisticated
stores that offered customers an expertly curated
collection of wines in Mumbai

Training the next generation: With students at
the Sonal Holland Academy

My greatest champions:
My parents, my sister Rimal, little
Rianna and Rimal's daughter Vinona,
on holiday in Dubai

The ones who are at the foundation of everything:
Daughter-in-law Gabrielle, stepson Chris, husband
Andrew, stepdaughter Charlotte and daughter Rianna
(left to right)

With the one who overcomes
all obstacles: Ganpati